WITHDRAWN FROM.

KT-406-729

KA 0015837 2

A
T
A

Evaluating and Assessing for Learning

Evaluating and Assessing for Learning

Duncan Harris and Chris Bell

Kogan Page, London/Nichols Publishing
Company, New York

Dedicated to all the learners and colleagues with whom we have been, are, and hope to be associated

First published in Great Britain in 1986 by Kogan Page Ltd
120 Pentonville Road, London N1 9JN

Copyright © Duncan Harris and Chris Bell 1986
All rights reserved

British Library Cataloguing in Publication Data

Harris, Duncan
　Evaluating and assessing for learning.
　1. Educational technology
　I. Title　　II. Bell, Chris
　371.3'07'8　　　LB1028.3

　ISBN 0-85038-991-7

First published in the USA in 1986 by Nichols Publishing Company
PO Box 96, New York, NY 10024

Library of Congress Cataloging-in-Publication Data

Harris, Duncan.
　Assessment and evaluation for learning.
　Bibliography: p.
　1. Learning.　　2. Educational tests and measurements.
3. Teaching.　I. Bell, Chris.　　II. Title.
LB1060.H37　　1986　　　370.15'23　　　85-28450
ISBN 0-89397-240-1

Printed and bound in Great Britain by
Billing & Sons Ltd, Worcester

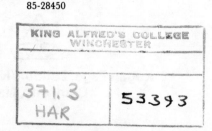
KING ALFRED'S COLLEGE
WINCHESTER

371.3
HAR

53393

CONTENTS

Section 5: Meeting the Needs of Learners

Acknowledgements

We would like to offer our thanks and appreciation to all those who have contributed in one way or another to the development of this book. To mention them all by name would be too daunting a task, but in particular we wish to thank:

— The learners and colleagues who over a long period of time have helped us form and develop our ideas.
— The people who have read through various parts of the text and commented so helpfully.
— Ray Winders for his contribution on audioconferencing.
— Our patient and long suffering publishers.
— Jan who spent many hours transforming the vagaries of our writing into readable text.

Duncan Harris
Chris Bell

Preface

Educational and training systems are moving away from the use of the human mind as a store for information, towards using the human mind for sorting, discriminating and using information which is already stored elsewhere. There is also a move away from assessing which is based on examinations taken on a particular day to classify, order and rank people, to assessing which looks for mastery and for records of personal achievements over a period of time. The onus for learning is being shifted from the teacher to the learner. The roles of teacher and learner are rapidly changing with the teacher being seen as a manager and organizer of learning rather than a presenter of knowledge.

In this book we consider the roles of learners and teachers. We have used the word 'learner' to indicate anyone who is in a learning situation; it could be a trainer finding out about new training methods, a teacher finding out about new assessment methods or the more obvious trainees, students and pupils (from high school/secondary school upwards). By 'teacher' we mean anyone organizing a learning experience for others; it could be a student organizing a syndicate with other students, a trainee presenting a case study or, once again, the more obvious lecturers, trainers, tutors or teachers.

The book is divided into five sections. Each section can be read independently. The order in which we have presented the sections is our preferred order, but we are conscious that other readers may prefer alternative orders. Cross-references to other sections are frequently given.

In order to make the reading of the book easier we have departed from the normal academic practice of giving references in the text. We have provided a short annotated list of further reading at the end of each section. References in these lists are intended for the reader who wants to take further a particular topic or idea we have introduced. In some cases, references present an alternative or complementary perspective to that which we have adopted. We have tried to acknowledge further sources of many of our ideas by including a bibliography at the end of the book. We apologize if we have inadvertently and unintentionally omitted other references. The omission is our responsibility.

Throughout the book we have included brief case studies known to us. Where we are aware of the case study being reported in the literature it is included in the bibliography.

We anticipate the readers of the book to include:

— mature students on advanced courses
— tutors of advanced courses
— groups of teachers undertaking curriculum development on a local or regional/county basis
— groups of trainers undertaking development of training materials.

Because we consider that more will be learned and experienced through being actively involved in learning, and we perceive the main readership as being professionals who are not working alone, we have included suggestions for group work at the end of each section.

Finally, we wish to note that the book gives the present views of the authors. Many colleagues, students and writers have contributed to these views, and we gratefully acknowledge their ideas. We realize that many alternative perspectives exist and do not intend what we have written to be taken as definitive; rather we hope to encourage people to think, discuss and try alternatives.

Section 1 Needs of the Learner

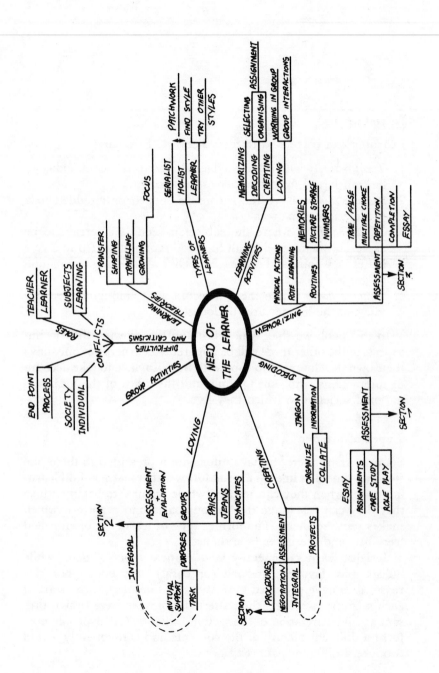

1. Needs of the Learner

Introduction

Learning can be related to four theories of teaching:

1. *Transfer theory* where knowledge is treated as a commodity to be transferred from one person to another.
2. *Shaping theory* where the learner is shaped or moulded to a predetermined pattern.
3. *Travelling theory* where the subject is seen as a terrain to be explored; the more difficult hills and mountains help to give a better viewpoint and the teacher is like a travelling companion or guide.
4. *Growing theory* where the intellectual and emotional development of the learner are the focuses.

In this book we shall concentrate on the growing theory, but aspects of the other three will be apparent. Learners not only have their own development to cope with but also have to take account of interactions with other people and the ethos of the local and national societies in which they live.

Types of learner

Some learners prefer to have information presented to them one step at a time in a linear or serial form. Other learners find learning easier when they can see the 'whole picture' to begin with so that they can rearrange the various parts into a pattern which makes sense to them. The former type of learner is often called 'serialist' and the latter type 'holist'.

Serialist learners generally favour linear types of notes while holists may favour patterned (or coral) type notes. For this reason, we have provided both styles of summary at the start of each section. However, the patterned notes we have drawn present our interpretation of the section contents. Other people may form a different picture of the contents and consequently would produce a different patterned note.

Many learners are able to switch from one style to the other, often according to the structure of the learning under consideration. Perhaps this ability to switch could be described as a 'patchwork' style. Some learners are only able to operate in one or other of the styles. Do we help them feel more secure with the other style, or do we adopt material and how it is used to the preferred styles of individual learners?

Learners may be unaware of their own preferred style and may need help in identifying that which is most comfortable for them. Some of the activities at the end of this section are designed to help identify the preferred learning styles of learners.

In order to encourage learners to try alternative styles, it is helpful if teachers can use varied strategies of notes and presentations, and persuade learners to try new methods, share their ideas with other learners and evaluate the strengths and weaknesses themselves. Some institutions adopt a policy of all teachers spending time on learning skills and study methods in relation to their own subjects. Other institutions give help during pastoral, tutorial or counselling activities. One of the author's institutions provides a series of free booklets on study skills to all its learners. The purpose is to help learners to gain confidence in their ability to learn, and therefore to learn more effectively.

We return to the ideas noted above in several parts of the book. In particular, learning how to learn is discussed on page 154.

Learning activities

Let us consider four members of the same family: Pat, Norma(n), Nick(y) and Jo(e). Jo(e) drives a fire engine, Norma(n) is a journalist, Pat is a coal miner operating equipment at the coal face and Nick(y) is a social worker. Each of them uses certain knowledge and routines which he/she has memorized; each of them has information and data which he/she has to decode and use; each of them has to create solutions to problems; and each of them has to work within a team. We suggest that, during learning, learners need to carry out a number of activities:

— memorizing
— decoding
— creating
— loving.

In a learning context, activity may be in the form of remembering by heart (memorizing), reading, selecting and organizing information to write an assignment (decoding), heuristic and creative activities (creating) and working within a group developing and facilitating group interactions (loving). Let us consider each of these learning activities in the context of a simplified learning experience.

A new stereo cassette deck, amplifier and speakers have been bought by a family. On unpacking the boxes, the family finds that there are no instructions for operating the cassette deck. On the front panel of the deck are a variety of push-button switches, each with a symbol. After connecting the equipment, the family discusses the meaning of the symbols. Each has his or her own ideas. Norma (whose present the deck is) not only attempts to decode the meaning of each symbol, but also has to decode the often conflicting ideas coming from the rest of the family.

Norma makes a series of decisions, and tries to operate the deck. Some decisions are correct (have the desired outcome) and others are wrong. Further decoding occurs in the light of her experiences. The meaning of symbols becomes clearer and can now be memorized by the whole family.

Jack has just learnt to read. To help him operate the deck, Norma creates a set of simple written labels which she sticks above the controls. Norma has decoded information from a variety of sources, memorized the use of the deck and has used this information to create an alternative set of instructions.

The stereo equipment now works. However, Jack wants his bedtime story tapes played, Norma wants to listen to some folk music, whereas both parents want to listen to classical music. The family needs to readjust to a new potential source of conflict: a loving activity!

We consider each of the learning activities in greater depth. They will be referred to at various parts of the book.

Memorizing

Drivers of taxi-cabs, buses and coaches in large cities are often required to pass a test of knowledge of streets and one-way systems. Such a test may be required annually. Pilots of passenger aircraft are required to remember routines both for regular activities and for emergencies. Musicians, typists and sportsmen are required to remember sequences and positions of body, hands and fingers to enhance speed and accuracy. Linguists need to learn vocabulary, and master grammar and syntax. Actors need to remember cues and lines. Lawyers need to remember case histories.

Many facets of our lives require immediate recall of facts, sequences of ideas, or physical actions. However, memorizing and rote learning are becoming less popular in current educational thinking, but there are still many requirements for memorizing; it is in the context of meaningful rote learning and memorizing that this section is elaborated.

The learner needs routines, changes to maintain interest, techniques for learning (which have to be adapted to each individual), assignments and assessment. The teacher needs to add to these interactions systematic evaluating of problems, successes, and new ideas in order to modify present and identify future strategies. It is clear that assignments, assessing and evaluating are a crucial part of the negotiated process of learning between teacher and learner. They are a part of the means of providing immediate short-term motivation for the learner, and feedback for learners and teachers.

In memorizing or rote learning of knowledge, a variety of strategies can be adopted, for example:

— *mnemonics* (eg, ROYGBIV colours of the visible spectrum: red, orange, yellow, green, blue, indigo, violet)
— *picture storage* (eg, where a familiar room/scene is remembered and facts are located in particular drawers, or on a particular tree)
— *using numbers* (eg, where the person remembers numbers better than words and associates ideas with number sequences in order to recall them).

These mechanisms are used in order to overcome the limitations of the human memory. In over-simplified terms the human mind can recall about seven different items for discrimination at any one time. In order to extend the memory we group, classify and cluster: remembering seven classes of things, the first is subdivided into, say, four, and so on. The classification needs to be relevant to the learner and to whatever is being learned (for example, many actors find lines easier to remember when they are associated with actions or intonations).

The types of assessment most applicable for memorizing include:

— true/false questions
— multiple-choice questions
— repetition (eg, being required to write in extended form that which is provided)

— completion questions
— essay questions where the assumption is recall.

For movement (psychomotor) learning, assessment may involve accurate repetition at increasing speeds or levels of control.

What seems to be important in meaningful rote learning is that the learning makes sense in relation to the experiences of the learner. The examples that we have given relate to people's means of employment or to enabling them to be allowed to do something (eg, drive a car). In providing a learning situation, a crucial aspect is that the organizer must know the existing cognitive or psychomotor structures for the individual learner (or at very worst for the group) and to use and build upon this. Without assessing and evaluating, co-operating and negotiating with learners, the jug is used to fill the glass with meaningless repetition.

Decoding

Decoding is a popular form of learning at some levels, particularly with younger children, in higher education and with learners learning on their own (what we have called mediated self-learning in Section 5). Imagine a typical learning situation in some institutions. At the end of a lecture, a set of problems are given out which are designed to build upon information presented during the lecture. A number of books and video recordings are mentioned as being useful to study before answering the problems.

The suggested books, lecture material and video recording all present information about the subject of the problems, but:

— several of the books are very complicated, each presenting different parts of the 'whole' picture
— two of the books appear to be in conflict over certain points
— the video recording only presents a small area of information; it was designed to be used as part of a distance study course.

Learners presented with the scenario described above are faced with a number of possibilities; for example they could:

— ask the teacher for clarification (the 'right answer');
— decode the various sources of information, perhaps using one source to help explain another; or
— give up, perhaps finding it too difficult or unmotivating to decode with a view to learning new information.

In the above example, decoding involves synthesizing information from different sources, perhaps discussing with fellow learners while so doing. Decoding is equally needed by many when presented with symbols (eg, map, tape deck), or complex or jargon-ridden information. For example:

In highly structured linear and cumulative subjects the decision algorithm is easier to control than those subjects where value judgements are involved.

or Plug type cup testers suitable for pressure testing the BOP equipment are installed on all casing strings.

or In some countries, people nod their heads meaning 'no' while shaking the head means 'yes'. A person from a country which uses nodding for yes will have to adapt. The decoding will take time.

All the above examples may require a considerable amount of decoding, depending upon the pre-knowledge of the reader: what is perfectly clear to the writer could be meaningless to the reader.

The process of finding information, ideas, evidence and collating and organizing these aspects is a complex task, often overlooked by the 'expert' teacher who has already been initiated. The style of assessing which is applicable for these needs of learners is different from those outlined in the previous part, although they obviously overlap, relate and share common techniques. Here, the focus of questions, essays or assignments will be on assessing the learner's ability to take and restructure information. 'Comprehension-type' assessment is a good example, where learners read (or watch) something and then have to interpret its meaning when answering questions. Case study and role play are also possibilities, particularly when body signals are important (for example in much foreign language teaching).

The driving test in the UK consists of several elements. The learner driver has to know off by heart the meaning of all the traffic signs and road markings in the Highway Code. In the test a selection of these are asked using miniature symbols. By memorizing the symbols and their meaning the learner should be able to pass this part of the test. The learner also has to be able to start and stop the car smoothly, do an emergency stop, reverse into a restricted-width opening or road, and turn the car round in a road (the three-point turn). All of these manoeuvres are memorized psychomotor sequences where practice enables satisfactory performance. Most of the remainder of the test is driving in normal traffic where decoding will be necessary because the conditions are unpredictable.

Seldom will the learner driver be required to act creatively unless he or she and the tester are strangers in the area (a case is known to one of the authors!).

Creating

Project work and creative work have been particularly used with younger age groups and in higher education. They have been less common in high schools/secondary schools except in certain creative subjects such as art and in the industrial arts and technologies.

In real life there are many occupations which obviously require this sort of expertise; there are also many where initiative is required but the educational system has prevented its development. The obvious examples are: artist, architect, and detective. There are also some less obvious ones: messenger, secretary, and taxi-cab driver.

Initiative, creative opportunities, and the need to search for resources relating to a topic of your own choice are associated much more with education up to the age of 11 years. After this age there is a tendency to move towards a subject-based education where the teacher becomes a subject expert rather than a pedagogic expert. The learner finds a different expectation where the requirement is to remember, to comprehend preconceived concepts or to accept existing critical review. Obviously this is an exaggerated picture of education and training after the age of 11, but it is still the prevalent view.

In learning situations which are aiming at creative or project-type work, where initiative and willingness to try out ideas are essential, the role of assessment is rather different from those roles already outlined. Generally the learner has a need for a lot of support and confidence boosting in the early stages, but that support needs to be gradually withdrawn. It sounds easy, but unfortunately learners have very different time-scales for this withdrawal of support. Some may require the support to be withdrawn fairly early in the process and a more critical view taken by the teacher. For others it may be difficult to persuade them to 'paddle their own canoes'.

The assessment becomes very much an integral part of the learning. There are a set of key questions that need to be asked early in the process:

1. What are the purposes of the learning experience?
2. What does the learner think are the purposes of particular work that has been agreed or allocated?

3. What are the purposes of the assessment procedure that has been agreed or negotiated?
4. What is the relationship between the learning experience and the assessment? (Has the assessment become the whole organization of the experience?)

The type of work outlined here is probably one of the most difficult to assess without losing sight of the purpose of learning. It would appear that very often negotiated contracts and agreements are one way of overcoming some of these difficulties and of providing motivation to the learner. However, there must be very careful consideration given to whether the assessment should be entirely associated with the end product or with the process, or even with both aspects. The assessment itself can also be viewed in a number of possible ways:

— impression
— objective
— contract
— ranking.

These are discussed further in Section 3.

Loving
Much work in real life is carried out by groups of people. Not only does the group have to do a particular series of tasks but also each member of the group needs to adjust to other members of the group. The educational system has not incorporated this as an important aspect except in certain specialist training in higher education (eg, psychology, management) where it is carried out at a fairly sophisticated level. However, we argue that it is an important and inherent need in any educational system and also in many aspects of training. Learners need to find out quite explicitly how to work in groups. The associated assessing and evaluating needs to take account of these requirements.

Work within groups can be considered to have the following purposes:

— to promote understanding of a body of knowledge
— to elucidate misunderstanding and difficulty
— to practise skills: intellectual, verbal, computational and social
— to practise application of principles in familiar and unfamiliar situations
— to explore personal professional attitudes and values
— to enable a two-way exchange of information.

It can be seen that these purposes cover everything from a pair of learners working out a mathematics problem together, to a group of people learning how best to work together as a team. One of the interesting things about working in groups (up to a size of about 16 in number) is the way that assessment and evaluation become a much more natural and integral part of the whole learning process rather than something that is added on as an extra and imposed from outside by a teacher or an external examining body.

In a very simplified form the group has two main functions:

1. The completion of a task within the limitations of the members of the group (a 'task-centred' function).
2. The mutual support within the group in order to carry out whatever task is in hand to the mutual satisfaction of the group (a 'process-centred' function).

It is crucial that a group learns that these are competing requirements and it is therefore necessary for the group to stay together as long as possible in order to get a feel of the learning requirements and of each other. We have made some suggestions about how groups can be encouraged to function in Section 2 (see page 46). It is recommended that some or all of these techniques are used with students whatever the learning or training area that they are involved in.

Considering the two types of group focus (task-centred and process-centred) let us consider more of the implications for, and needs of, the learners. The task-centred group will focus on such aspects as:

— the application of principles
— acquiring and practising skills (this could include the skills of working in a group)
— promoting understanding (for example why work as an individual when the discussion and argument with other learners may help to overcome learning difficulties? But the learners need to change their attitude that learning and life are all about being competitive and secretive; there are social as well as educational implications.)

The process-centred group will focus more on the following aspects:

— the understanding of interpersonal interaction
— the development of group skills
— the development of professional skills in communication

— the understanding of personal bias
— exploratory or creative problem solving.

The characteristics shown by members of a group in the task-centred area will be communication, evaluation and control. It should be immediately clear that the two focuses overlap. The recognition of members' perspectives and roles in the task area can be seen by activities such as giving suggestions, giving opinions, asking for opinions, asking for suggestions and giving or asking for orientation.

The characteristics of the process-centred approach are decision making, tension reduction, and group integration. Recognition would be by looking for antagonism, solidarity, tension and tension release, agreement and disagreement. It should be clear that different learners will have different needs according to their previous experiences. It becomes necessary for the individual and other members of the group to identify each learner's needs as far as possible, rather than using a continuous series of interventions from the teacher. However, the skills and methods of working in a group cannot be assumed, they must be nurtured. Because the learner's view of learning is coloured by previous experience there will be a clear need to enable the group to function more efficiently in this mode.

> A group of teachers attending an in-service course on evaluating were asked to write down briefly how they used assessment in their own school. In pairs each member introduced him/herself with a very brief outline of the school. Pairs then looked for differences in what each had previously written. In fours, groups tried to identify any consensus. In the process so far the learners (in this case teachers) were finding out and learning from one another.
>
> The course leaders now asked each group of four to report one use for assessment. Uses were recorded on the overhead projector, and the process was continued until all were identified. Now not only were the learners hearing about other people's views but also the course leaders (ie, the teachers) were finding out where the course members were in their thinking, so that the course could be built on those bases rather than either repeating ground already familiar or jumping too far ahead. The process enabled the course leaders to identify the prerequisites while also encouraging the learners to learn from one another in their first meeting.

(Further details of this technique (snowballing) are given in Section 2.)

Suggested group activities

1. *What is good learning and bad learning?*
The question is used as a basis for the group to exchange and

23

share ideas. In order to help the group, raise the two ideas separately. For example: 'think of a good learning experience that you have had', 'think of a bad learning experience you have had'. In order to help them to focus their ideas it is worth saying that these experiences can be in any context (eg, hobbies or school). Use snowballing, nominal group technique or buzz groups to help the group discussion (see Section 2 for further details of these techniques).

2. *How do you take notes?*
Ask learners to bring notes with them and go into pairs immediately to explain to one another why they took their notes that way and how they will use them. After about ten minutes ask the group to move into fours (as in snowballing). Ask them to identify good and bad practice in taking notes.

3. *How do you use your time?*
A series of questions can be given to each learner. The learners are asked to mark those that apply to them. When individuals have completed their list they move into pairs and compare with another learner looking for differences. On completion of this, fours are asked to identify whether each question matters and to come to some sort of consensus on the use of time. Fours report in the normal way for snowballing (see page 47). This approach is described in detail in Gibbs (1981).

4. *How do you develop your own information system?*
Ask learners to bring their own system (eg, a card or computer index of references they have found valuable) and explain it to another learner. After this they move into fours looking for good and bad characteristics of information systems. Reporting is carried out in the normal way.

5. *How important is social interaction?*
A paper may be given to the learners for them to read before they meet. At the meeting, learners are not permitted to criticize the paper. The first stage is to identify any parts of the paper that cannot be understood or which are considered to need clarification. The learners then explain their difficulties to one another. The procedure goes on to identify the main issues in the paper, to discuss these individually, the way in which the paper fits into the group member's own experience, and the application of the paper

in the present context. Only then can the paper be criticized, and the group can look at its own performance.

This method is called 'learning through discussion'; see Hill (1978) for further details.

6. *How do learners differ?*
A free discussion on Section 1 of this book could be used.

7. *Learner at home, tutor at home, learner wants help. How can the help be arranged?*
Either use role play, where pairs argue out the basis between themselves and then report their suggestions to the rest of the group, or use brainstorming (see page 49).

Difficulties and criticisms

There are basic educational conflicts in the ideas that have been outlined in this chapter. The behavioural and contractual type of learning tends to assume an end-point specification where the product is assessed. So, for example, if a learner is given a project to do with a period of time in which to complete it, then the end-point approach will only assess the report or the artefact that comes at the end of the process. However, in the process-type of approach the assessment would focus primarily on the way in which the problem was approached, the stategies used, the decisions made, the basis of those decisions, the evaluation of alternative strategies, etc.

Is education about developing the individual or ensuring that the individual fits into society? The former will focus on the attributes, strengths and weaknesses of the individual without attempting to mould that individual, whereas the latter will want to mould the individual into conformity. Perhaps the classic dilemma is in teacher training: is the teacher to be trained to fit into the existing system (the 'sitting by Nellie' approach), developed as an individual to work to the best of his or her ability within his or her own personality, or even to be a radical change agent for society? Obviously these have totally different assessment assumptions. The first example can be transferred into any aspect of learning where the learner is expected to follow and learn what is prescribed (at worst rote learning of existing ideas and concepts); the second example could be where an attempt is made to enable the learner to adapt his or her learning style to fit his or her own needs and there would not be an expectation of rote learning; the third example may be where the learner is required to question the whole basis of the subject or learning.

We have suggested a style of learning based on negotiation. This style is fine with willing learners, but what about unwilling and unmotivated learners? Unfortunately the change in approach is often introduced to learners who are already alienated from learning. Both categories of learners will need a lot of help initially in order to take on responsibility for their own learning because the general trend is still towards providing prepackaged learning whether on the chalkboard, in handouts, in books or in computer packages.

A teacher has to be a problem solver with a group of human beings, yet much teacher training is still carried out in a didactic mode to serried rows of learners in lecture theatres, with little attention paid to heuristic methods of learning. At the end of their teacher training course they will have to take on the responsibility for their own problem solving for which they have had little in the way of training or education.

Negotiated learning also depends on who is the major partner in the negotiation: who decides on the content, level, means of learning, time to be spent, assessment etc? Certification is also a problem; can negotiated learning be acceptable in external certification? Certainly, while the focus on certification is on competitive assessment there is some difficulty in negotiating, except as the best way to beat the assessors! However, with a movement towards criterion-referenced measurement and towards profiles of achievement there is more potential for negotiated learning.

The development of the learner as identified above involves decisions about the learner's strengths and weaknesses. Who controls the building on the strengths and building up from the weaknesses? Assessment has a key role to play in this process. Caution should be exercised, however, as there is not sufficient evidence to support the idea that teacher-developed assessment procedures can pinpoint actual learner weaknesses by themselves. In a subject such as mathematics, there may be several different ways (or algorithms) of devising the answer to a particular question. Where simple questions (eg, multiple-choice) are used, only one of these algorithms may have been taken into account in the grading scheme; the learner who uses a different algorithm may well have incorrect diagnosis of errors.

In a negotiated learning situation assessment is not remote from the learner but something about which the learner and the teacher talk, the learner identifying the sort of strategies that they have taken. If it appears that the time involved in such negotiation is beyond the staff-learner ratio, then the learners themselves can take some of the responsibility for part of their own assessment. In this case it is important that the teacher does see learners' work on a systematic and regular basis.

Another key area of difficulty is the influence of the subject or discipline. The learner is involved in the process of learning; that process depends on his or her own stage of development and also on his or her previous experience. Unfortunately much subject-based learning does not take into account the development of the learner. The subject is constructed around content, concepts, and frameworks. It is taught in a fixed time-scale, often ignoring the development of the learner, and at worst in a lock-step time-oriented basis. The learning may be more suitable for a fixed learning variable time basis, but this requires a totally different idea of the organization of teaching and assessment. It is often assumed that only mastery-type learning is suitable for a variable time approach. There are many distance study courses around the world in a complete range of disciplines. Few of these operate on a fixed time basis in the way that institutionalized education and training do. Why should the people on distance study courses have that type of learning almost exclusively for themselves? What is the potential in institutionalised education and training?

Annotated bibliography

Anania, J (1983)
The Influence of Instructional Conditions on Student Learning and Achievement
Evaluation in Education, 7, 1, 1–92.

This long paper identifies a study carried out in an American school. The focus of the study was the human potential for learning. The study identified that most learners had a great capacity for learning. Three styles of learning environment were considered — conventional teaching, mastery learning and a tutoring approach. The latter two approaches which are elaborated involved high participation by learners, cues to and evidence of success. 'Almost every' student had a very high capacity for learning once they identified a belief in their own ability. The two approaches depended heavily on assessment for learning.

Ausubel, D P, Novak, J D and Hanesian, H (1978)
Educational Psychology: a Cognitive View
New York: Holt, Rinehart and Winston.

A detailed discussion of the ways in which individuals learn. The book provides much information of direct relevance to improving the quality of learning, from structuring learning materials and aids to analysing learning styles.

Bawden, R and Valentine, I (1984)
Learning to be a Capable Systems Agriculturalist
Programmed Learning & Educational Technology, 21, 4, 273–87.

The course described focuses not only on systems agriculturalists but also on those agriculturalists being autonomous learners and effective communicators, aimed at helping others and building up good interpersonal relationships. The course uses two learning strategies in two contexts. The contexts are staff initiative (gradually decreasing) and student initiative (gradually increasing); the latter involves the use of co-operative groups. The assessment is based around a student- and employer-initiated competency profile including peer and self-evaluation of learning.

Bloom, B S *et al.* (1956)
Taxonomy of Educational Objectives Handbook 1: Cognitive Domain
New York: McKay.

A proposal for a taxonomy based on the analysis of a large number of assessments at various levels of education in the USA. The framework of the basic six levels is knowledge, comprehension, application, analysis, synthesis and evaluation. Examples of objectives and assessments are given in the book.

Buzan, T (1982)
Use Your Head
London: BBC Publications.

The book explains discoveries about the human brain and helps the reader to understand more clearly how human minds work. It includes tests and exercises to improve reading power, memory, studying effectively, solving problems more readily and ways of thinking. The well known mind maps (otherwise known as coral diagrams, patterned notes, etc) are a feature of the book.

Entwistle, N (1981)
Styles of Teaching & Learning: An Integrated Outline of Educational Psychology
London: Wiley.

Provides an overview of those aspects of educational psychology related to an understanding of how learners learn. The book is a good starting place for someone new to this area of psychology or who wants a summary of research findings. Many references are provided.

Fox, D (1983)
Personal Theories of Education
Studies in Higher Education, 8, 2, 151–63.

This paper provides the basis of the first paragraph of the section with four theories of teaching: transfer theory, shaping theory, travelling theory, and growing theory.

Gagné, R M (1976)
The Conditions of Learning
New York: Holt, Rinehart and Winston.

Expounds the use of a particular learning hierarchy which can be used to analyse learning and the curriculum. Ideas presented provide useful starting points when considering how to structure learning aids and materials to improve learning.

Gibbs, G (1981)
Teaching Students how to Learn: a Student Centred Approach
Milton Keynes: Open University Press.

The focus is on students learning from one another. By learning from peers with the same problems on the same course, the gap between them is less than that between most students and tutors. Examples are provided for carrying out the process, often using a 1:2:4 snowball approach.

Hill, W F (1978)
Learning Thru' Discussion
Palo Alto: Feareon.

A small book which gives a ten-stage system for organizing discussion particularly related to discussion around papers that are provided. The system involves focusing on problems of comprehension and the main messages of the paper, leaving the criticism until near the end. The final focus is on the group's performance.

Honey, P and Mumford, A (1982)
The Manual of Learning Styles
Maidenhead: Peter Honey.

A manual aimed particularly at managers, but of interest to all learners. The authors suggest four learning styles: activists, reflectors, theorists and pragmatists. The characteristics of all are elaborated and a questionnaire is provided to enable learners to classify their own styles. The manual aims to enable learners to develop as all-rounders.

Jonassen, D H (1985)
Learning Strategies: A New Educational Technology
Programmed Learning & Educational Technology, 22, 1, 26–34.

The paper addresses the more cognitive theories and assumptions and their implementation in educational technology. The failure to provide generalizable instructional techniques has forced us to shift our emphasis to what learners do. Educational technologies need to become learner-oriented. The goal of new technologies, such as learning strategies, is to promote independent, self-motivated learners who are capable of initiating, selecting, and using appropriate strategies for acquiring, retaining and using knowledge.

Section 2 Evaluating: Fitting the System to the Needs of Learners

2. Evaluating: Fitting the System to the Needs of Learners

Introduction

Throughout the text we are emphasizing learning as a co-operative venture between 'learner' and 'teacher'. Nowhere is such co-operation more important than in the evaluation process which we consider should be an integral part of course design, implementation and post-course reflection. Traditionally the before, during and after phases of learning have been given the labels 'needs analysis', 'formative evaluation' and 'summative evaluation'.

Needs analysis (or preparatory evaluation) is a necessary part of course design, although often discussed less in educational than training environments. Needs analysis is as important when considering an individual lesson or seminar as it is when designing a new distance learning package. Mismatch between the learner and content or approach of learning is unlikely to optimize learning and may well lead to alienation. As we move towards open and self-learning, then needs analysis becomes increasingly important for the learners to undertake themselves: what do I need to learn? what do I want to learn? how may I best learn?

Evaluating during the learning process (often termed formative evaluation) is important for learners and teachers alike, aiding the teacher in fine-tuning (or hole plugging and patching) and the learner in becoming more involved in, and aware of, the learning process. In addition, the communication which should arise naturally from such evaluation is a vital aid to the learners and teachers becoming more aware both of themselves and of each other's views, problems and expectations; it should be a sharing process.

Evaluating subsequent to learning (often termed summative evaluation) is necessary for providing information to both learners and teachers about learning which has occurred, perhaps comparing it with that which was intended. Factors enabling and constraining the learning process may also be identified. Such evaluating can provide the learner and teacher with information

35

about what learning is still necessary to achieve particular goals, and the teacher about development of future courses.

In this section we discuss the processes of planning and organizing evaluating and consider various styles and techniques which can be used at the different phases of learning. Throughout, emphasis is on small-scale applications where the aim is understanding and improving learning/teaching. For readers who require further details of techniques sign-posted in this section, texts noted in the bibliography at the end should form useful starting points.

Processes, planning and purposes of evaluating

Many processes which we would place under the broad umbrella of 'evaluating' arise naturally and spontaneously during learning. Examples of such evaluating could be:

— The puzzled faces and body language of learners in a workshop who have just been asked by the organizer to undertake some task or other which indicate that more explanation of the task is needed.
— The teacher developing computer-aided assessment techniques asks her son to try out the program while she observes and later discusses problems with him.
— The mathematician who, in a 'problems class', notices the same learning difficulty for many learners and calls together the whole group for additional discussion and help.

Likewise, evaluation at the more formal end of the spectrum could be a planned, highly organized and time-consuming evaluation of a new multi-media distance learning package. In this case, the evaluation is likely to be undertaken within a fixed time, possibly aimed at bringing about change; throughout this book, we suggest evaluating as an ongoing process.

Planning, methods and outcomes are likely to appear very different in the above sets of examples, but each involves the collection and analysis of information to help make informed judgements about how worthwhile something is. In each case, cultural and sociological value judgements have to be made. In a learning context, each of the processes will have (or at least should have) the improvement of learning as one of its major goals.

Although the examples used above may appear to have definite starting and ending points, only a snapshot has been taken; in reality we consider that the process of evaluating should be a continuous and ongoing integral part of the total organization and practice of learning.

Let us consider the teacher developing the computer-assisted assessment. The process may be something like this:

1. The teacher spends much time marking multiple-choice questions designed to assess the mastery of particular skills. Because of the time needed to mark questions, feedback to individual learners is usually a week after they have completed their practicals and questions about these. Only then can remedial action be planned between teacher and learner.
2. The 'problem' is discussed with learners and colleagues. Methods used in other parts of the institution, and outside, are observed and evaluated. Needs are analysed.
3. Alternatives are discussed. A specification is drawn up, taking due account of constraints. Computer-'generated' and marked test items are decided upon. Learners will be provided with immediate feedback and results are easily noted for later analysis by the teacher.
4. The teacher evaluates existing systems and decides to purchase and modify one of these. The new system is tested, first at home during development and later within the laboratory. The feedback is provided by learners and colleagues which leads to 'fine-tuning' of the system.
5. The system is used by all learners. As they use it, they are observed and later asked to comment about it.
6. Because the analysis of specific learning difficulties is now easier, it is apparent that certain of the laboratory techniques are not being successfully mastered. This forms the starting point of further evaluating.

There are a number of identifiable stages in the above process. In practice these are not likely to have clearly definable boundaries but will blur into each other:

1. An issue (need or problem) arises.
2. The issue is analysed, discussed, thought about. Needs, expectations and hopes are identified.
3. A way forward is arrived at in the light of information collected from various sources. It is decided to make changes.
4. The changes are implemented.
5. The new technique is monitored closely in use for its effects and effectiveness, thus enabling the changes to be evaluated.
6. The change leads to identification of further issues/problems.

Figure 2.1

Throughout, importance was placed on negotiating and communicating, keeping those involved informed and seeking their help and advice.

Viewed in this way, the process of evaluating can be considered to be an ongoing spiral as shown in Figure 2.1. We do not intend this spiral to be prescriptive, but rather to indicate one particular model for evaluating. The model can be applied to many styles of evaluating, but is perhaps most applicable when discussing small-scale evaluating, or self-evaluating, as we are concerned with here.

As can be seen from Figure 2.1, we consider the collecting and analysing of information to be central to the process of evaluating; therefore, the majority of this section is set aside to describe various techniques of collecting information, particularly those most applicable to small-scale processes aimed at helping learners learn. For convenience, we have divided these techniques into: listening and talking; observing; and pencil and paper.

Styles of evaluating

In evaluating, as in most activities, the same 'problem' can be approached from a variety of viewpoints using a variety of approaches. We will not discuss the various theoretical or philosophical assumptions underlying different approaches towards evaluating; the reader interested in this area is directed to one of the sources noted in the bibliography at the end of this section. Here, we merely indicate four possible approaches to a common problem using a fictitious case study.

In a certain city, the buses were constantly criticized by the public: they never ran on time and drivers were rude. The bus company decided to call on four expert evaluators to find out what was wrong and to make suggestions about how matters could be improved.

The first evaluator decided that the problem was due to the male chauvinistic attitude of the drivers. He produced an operational description (or hypothesis) of the problem and proceeded to test this definition. He developed an attitude scale comprising a large number of statements on a questionnaire. Questionnaires were handed out to all bus passengers over the period of a week. The evaluator analysed the data using a large computer. His report indicated that the problem was not due to a male chauvinistic attitude among drivers.

The second evaluator also thought that the problem was due to drivers' attitudes. He developed an open-ended questionnaire after consultation with a sample of passengers and drivers. The questionnaire was given to passengers and drivers over a period of a week. Analysis of the questionnaire responses in a report provided some useful pointers to the bus company about how to improve their service.

The third evaluator decided that her area of interest was in the interactions between passengers and drivers. She travelled on many buses over a long period, talking to passengers and drivers. She also spoke with several members of the management. During early discussions, she identified several issues of importance to those with whom she spoke, and used these to devise questions to ask during interviews. A series of short reports were written during the evaluation which formed the focus of discussions between drivers, management and a sample of passengers. The process of evaluating increased communication and helped those people involved to share their experiences and ideas. The final report provided useful information. The bus service was much improved.

The fourth person approached the 'problem' in a different way. He spent each day travelling with one driver, getting to know the driver and many of the passengers very well. The passengers and the driver were encouraged to discuss and explore their feelings, openly sharing their ideas and criticisms. As a result, the driver changed his attitude a great deal, he became very popular with his passengers and an excellent service was provided on his bus.

Bias of information

Two people describing a particular event will generally provide two different accounts. It is often pointless to think along the lines of 'who is giving the most accurate answer?' or 'who observed the situation correctly?'. One of the authors remembers all too well watching, together with a colleague, a video recording of a teacher with a group of learners. Later, both made notes about what was seen: good points, points which could be improved and overall impressions. On comparison, the notes described two very different learning situations. Someone reading these notes without also knowing the context would be unlikely to realize that they both described the same classroom at the same time seen through the same camera lens!

The above example is perhaps extreme, but it did occur. When collecting information from people, one should remember that what is collected is unlikely to represent an objective reality. Rather, the information represents an individual's perceptions of reality at the particular time information is collected. Perceptions are likely to depend upon a large number of factors, for example:

— the individual's view of the 'world'
— the approach adopted to collecting information
— the way in which any questions are asked (or written)
— the rapport between 'supplier' and 'collector'.

Add to this possible bias or distortion during recording the information ('I hear what I like to hear') and during analysing and summarizing ('I note what I want to note'), and the need for thought and care is obvious.

Approaching the same situation from a number of viewpoints, or using a number of information collectors or techniques generally helps reduce bias. Such approaches are called 'triangulation' (further details are given on page 66). Feeding information back to the person or group who initially supplied it so that it can be checked and commented upon is often a valuable technique, even if time consuming. Not only does this reduce bias during recording and summarizing, but it also gives the respondent a chance of later reflection upon what he or she said.

The need for planning and purpose

Whatever the focus or style of evaluating, there is a need for it to have a purpose and generally for it to have a plan. These may be very specific or broad. Nebulous ideas will often be focused into more specific plans as the evaluating process progresses. There is no harm in this. Questions to be asked, discussed and borne in mind when thinking about and undertaking evaluating include:

— What do we hope to achieve?
— How can the important issues be identified?
— Who should be involved in negotiating?
— What may be the effects of evaluating?
— How can communication be maintained?
— How can information be collected and analysed?
— Who can best collect and analyse information?
— What are the most applicable sources of information?
— What are the constraints (eg, time, manpower, political)?

It may be useful to draw up a checklist using the above questions as headings and to discuss them with colleagues and learners. (See page 64 for details of checklists, and the activities at the end of this section for group activities.)

Using information from evaluating

It should be remembered that there must be a purpose for evaluating, for collecting information. In our context, this purpose is likely to be the improvement of learning/teaching, perhaps matching the needs and learning styles of learners to the systems of teaching. Very often the outcome of evaluating will be discussion between those involved: the 'evaluator', the learners and the teachers/organizers. Information collected should be seen as facilitating discussion, helping those involved to share and become more aware of each other's needs, perspectives and perceptions. It should encourage what we have described in Section 1 as creative and loving learning activities for all those involved. We recognize that this is often not the purpose of many evaluations. Perhaps it is a reason why many evaluations are held in low esteem by those at their focus.

Needs analysis

In most cases the learning content, sequence and environment are chosen by teachers and trainers. The decisions are often based on the opinions of those teachers or trainers sometimes using ideas generated from government agencies, researchers or the requirement of employers. Unfortunately, young learners or young trainees are from a different generation. Employers, who have been successful in a materialistic world, view their educational and training experience as either being essential (if they had good experiences) or as being disastrous; their views on education and training are usually conservative. Learners are seldom included in decision making about their own course, yet there can be an experiential difference between their background and that of the adults involved in organizing the learning.

There is a basis for discussion between learners, teachers, employers and immediate past learners. Not only do such discussions generate the expectations and objectives but also the problems and the assumptions which are relevant for all parties. Details of methods of setting up procedures for such discussions are considered later. However, we wish to emphasize that discussion and negotiation are essential parts of each course. Time spent in carrying out the process will reduce alienation and the ensuing motivation will soon enable time to be gained in a formal learning context. The results of discussions should be written up as a brief report and a copy held by all those involved with the course, including learners.

It may be that the course members and/or those organizing the course may wish to alter the original agreement as the course progresses, particularly if the course is of considerable duration. Opportunities for the original group members to meet and renegotiate the agreement should be built into the course. Modification should again be circulated to all involved. There may be constraints on the room for negotiation for externally validated courses, but even these do not preclude the process. In order to help learners to identify their needs it may be necessary to provide a mechanism for the group to exchange experiences of learning (see Section 1), whether they know one another or not. Those experiences will involve means of coping with assessment and examinations too. The views of each of those involved can be considered in a circle of activity (see Figure 2.2).

All learners start with themselves and their past experiences of life: home, learning, peer group and social pressures. The discussion leading to the course is a form of generation of an individual project. The course is the encounter! The experiences, learning and interpersonal activities lead to continual communication changing the person's being. This may be seen as a useful model for learners to take on more responsibility for their own learning. Their needs evolve from the continuous cycling of the loop.

We shall now consider some of the means of collecting information which lead to the identification of needs. We cannot emphasize too strongly that different individuals and different groups will have different needs. Identification of individual and group needs is an essential part of the learning process.

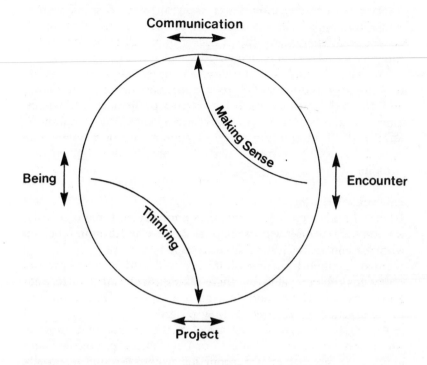

Figure 2.2

Listening and talking techniques

If learning is to be a co-operative venture between 'learner' and 'teacher' then there is a need for the two groups to have meaningful communication: such communication is often achieved effectively during discussion between those involved. We wish to emphasize an obvious, but often neglected point: one generally gleans more information by talking *with* rather than talking *to*. Therefore 'listen and talk' rather than 'talk and listen'!

Like the majority of information-gathering techniques, listening and talking can be organized at a variety of levels and can take many forms. It can:

— be informal or formal
— be non-structured or highly structured
— take place naturally or be specifically organized.

For example, considering individual 'interviews', the spectrum ranges from informal discussion, perhaps better described as a 'conversation with a purpose', to the formal and highly structured interview where the interviewer seeks answers to specific questions. Both approaches, and all those in between have their place: an informal 'chat over a cup of coffee' may well be as valuable as a highly organized and structured set of formal interviews.

We have divided listening and talking techniques into: informal discussions (one-to-one or groups); one-to-one interviews; and group discussions. Each has its own particular uses, advantages and disadvantages. As always when evaluating, it is important that the technique and approach adopted is chosen paying due regard to needs, purposes and the context of the particular situation.

Informal discussions

Informal discussion frequently arises naturally and spontaneously, but may also be planned, perhaps at the level of 'drop in for a cup of coffee and a chat'. Such discussions may have no preconceived focus or apparent purpose, but may well lead to the raising of issues or problems, allowing those taking part to air their feelings and ideas in a relaxed and informal atmosphere. Discussions can be 'sharpened' or focused as they progress.

Although often considered a tool of the 'evaluator', informal discussion with no 'organizer' or 'evaluator' present is most valuable in the context of improving learning. Groups of learners meeting during a coffee break may well discuss their learning. Much good can be done, both in facilitating group support and in raising issues of real relevance to the group. On the more negative side, discussions may degenerate into little more than 'shouting' sessions or personal rhetoric.

A skilled and sensitive 'interviewer' can collect much valuable information during informal discussions. The method is often a good starting point in collecting information, whether it be about planning new learning, discussing learning in progress, or reflecting upon that which has taken place. Ideas and issues raised may well form the basis of further investigation.

Individual interviews

We use the term 'interview' to indicate a method which is definitely planned by someone who has a purpose in collecting information. Interviews may be structured, partially structured or non-structured. Some ways of recording information during interviews are noted on page 51.

Structured interviews

Structured interviews involve the interviewer asking specific pre-defined questions. These questions should be carefully planned and written. They often require yes-no, or very brief answers. The interviewer usually has a checklist of questions on which the answers are recorded (see page 64).

Although used frequently for some purposes (eg, market research), structured interviews which allow little latitude for the respondent are of limited use as a technique for collecting information in the context of this book. Where straightforward factual information which requires little thought is required, then questionnaires are often the most applicable method, particularly if there is a large number of respondents. (Further details about questionnaires are given on page 58.) However, interviews which use structured questions as starting points for later elaboration are most appropriate. These are considered below.

Partially structured interviews

Partially structured interviews allow the respondent more freedom and latitude than structured interviews. The interviewer is likely to have an interview schedule or checklist of questions and issues he or she wishes to raise. These are used during the interview to generate discussion, and should be viewed as facilitating rather than inhibiting responses.

Partially structured interviews are a very useful technique of information collecting in the context of improving learning. They take advantage of the flexibility of non-structured techniques, while being easier for the interviewer to maintain the desired focus.

New staff in an institute of higher education attend an 'induction course'. Evaluating the effectiveness of the course is undertaken part-way through and at the end. Results from these evaluations help inform changes to the present course and help in the design of future courses.

One technique used to collect information is the partially structured interview. A schedule of issues to be raised during interviews is drawn up in consultation with the students and the staff who teach the course. These issues range from the broad and open (eg, 'Do you consider that the course has been useful to you?') to the more specific (eg, 'How long have you spent discussing teaching with your head of department?'). The latter type of question usually generates far more information than that specifically asked for.

During the interview, information is recorded using patterned notes (see page 52). Information is used to generate a summary for each person interviewed. Summaries are checked by the respondent for accuracy and further comment before being synthesized into a short written report.

Partially structured interviews need to be planned carefully before the interview. Planning may involve:

1. Deciding on the issues to be raised.
2. Deciding how to record information.
3. Writing questions and follow-up probes.
4. Trying out questions and probes on a few people from a group similar to those you are planning to interview.
5. Rewriting any questions which are ambiguous, difficult to answer or do not appear to provide what is being asked for.

Non-structured interviews
As distinct from what we have called informal discussions, non-structured interviews are carefully planned, have a definite purpose (this could be broad or very specific) and should be undertaken by someone who has practice and skill in the technique.

Used with care, non-structured interviews can yield information which may not emerge by use of other methods. The interviewer can respond to aspects raised by the respondent, and probe these in depth, often returning to them from a different viewpoint or from a different perspective. This approach to collecting information should not be undertaken lightly. A person with little experience of interviewing is best advised to use a more structured technique. As experience and confidence is gained then often movement towards less structured approaches is possible.

Group discussions
Group discussions have a number of advantages and disadvantages compared with one-to-one interviews. Advantages include:

1. The possibility of obtaining information from more people in less time.
2. Group interaction which may encourage individuals to feed off and build upon each other's comments.

A group discussion organized by an experienced and skilful person may help certain more reticent individuals to participate and give more than they otherwise would.

Potential disadvantages include:

1. The possible inhibiting effect upon some individuals, particularly if the discussion is conducted in a less than skilful manner.

2. Over-dominance by the more vociferous or articulate members of the group, leading the direction of discussion and inhibiting contribution by others.
3. The ease with which focus may be lost.

As noted in the introduction, group discussions may be organized in a non-structured or in a structured way. Non-structured group discussions have an important role, particularly in the early stages of identifying thoughts of the group concerned. However, this approach may lead to vague and unfocused discussion and may be an inefficient technique of collecting information in the later stages of evaluating. Once again, when planning a group discussion, we stress the need to consider carefully the purposes and aims of the exercise (see page 40). For example, if it is considered important to reduce the effects of the last two disadvantages noted above, then certain structuring techniques described below are useful.

Whatever form the group discussion takes, it is usually necessary to initiate it in some way. However, there may be times when group discussion arises naturally and spontaneously; these may be most fruitful! Some ways of initiating a group discussion include:

1. Group members can be asked a question.
2. A problem can be posed to the group.
3. The leader can introduce the main issues and chair the ensuing discussion; issues may be broad or very specific.
4. Examples, or case studies, can be presented for the group to discuss. Presentation may be verbal, visual or using written documents, perhaps distributed prior to the meeting. A video recording of the group in a learning situation could be shown (see also page 57).
5. One of the structuring techniques described below may be used.

Structuring discussion using the snowball technique
In essence, snowballing involves individuals personally focusing upon specific issues. Thoughts about these are first shared with small groups and later the whole group. The technique facilitates the maintenance of focus upon specific issues, and encourages each member of the group to be actively involved, while also allowing open discussion and interaction.

An example of the use of the technique is given below.

1. All members of the group are asked to write comments in

response to a question or issue. The question or issue may be presented verbally or could be written, perhaps in the form of an open questionnaire.

While individuals are working, the organizer does a rough count to decide how to put together pairs and later fours. If numbers do not divide, it may be necessary to use threes and fives etc.

2. Individuals form pairs to discuss and look for differences in their comments. As individuals appear to finish their notes (perhaps after five minutes or so), the organizer persuades the prospective partner to finish, and to join together to discuss each other's notes. If pairs do not know each other, they can be asked to introduce themselves.

3. Pairs join to form fours for further discussion. Once again, when pairs appear to be finishing their discussions (perhaps after five or ten minutes) the organizer uses the same process to bring together groups of four, asking them to look for consensus and possibly differences in what they have written and discussed previously. Groups may be asked to change direction at this stage and should be asked to nominate a spokesperson for later feedback.

4. When one group appears to have finished discussions (perhaps after 10 to 15 minutes) the organizer goes around all groups asking them to be ready to report back in five minutes. It is worth having a small extra activity available for groups who finish early.

5. Each group of four presents its findings to the whole group. The organizer may ask each group in turn for one comment only. These are recorded for all to see. When no further comments are forthcoming, the group may discuss, synthesize and evaluate findings.

As an alternative, snowballing may be organized by allowing the complete group specific times for each of the phases. Although possibly being easier to organize and 'control', keeping the group together tends to lose spontaneity and an individual approach to the work.

Information may be recorded by the techniques noted on page 51. Use may also be made of the notes written by individuals in the first part of the exercise.

Structuring discussion using the nominal group technique
Nominal group technique (NGT) is a variation of snowballing

and retains similar advantages. A typical NGT procedure is as follows:

1. The group leader identifies a question, or issues, designed to delineate clearly the scope of the inquiry yet giving individuals sufficient freedom for their own answers or suggestions.
2. Individuals write their own responses. Cards can be used which may later be collected by the group leader.
3. If cards are used to record individuals' comments, these can be dislayed for the group to read, or may be copied to acetate, flip-chart or board. Alternatively, the group leader may ask each person in turn to supply one answer or comment. The process is repeated until no further comments are forthcoming. Comments are noted by the group leader for all to see. At this stage no discussion is allowed.
4. Under the direction of the group leader, comments are classified, ordered and synthesized by the group. Discussion should help clarify meanings and establish the reasons for inclusion in the list. If information is of a more quantifiable nature, the group may be asked to rank issues in order of importance.
5. The group leader may encourage final discussion about the issues raised.

Structuring discussion by brainstorming
Brainstorming is a useful way of generating a range of ideas relatively quickly from a group of about 10 to 20 members. Organized sensitively, it overcomes some of the potential problems noted on page 46.

The group (or sub-groups within the whole) is asked a question or presented with a specific issue or problem. Each member is encouraged to give a short and spontaneous response irrespective of how far-fetched. Responses are recorded by the organizer and at this stage no discussion is allowed. In this way, novel and unusual ideas and comments are not discouraged by possible peer pressure. When no further responses are forthcoming, suggestions are discussed, synthesized and evaluated by the group. The key factors in a brainstorming session are:

1. The initial question or issue: it should be presented in a lively and clear way to help 'warm up' the group.
2. The group's initial responses: the group should be encouraged to let go of inhibitions and barriers — a 'free-wheeling' approach.

3. Suspend judgement: during the initial response, analysis and evaluation should not be allowed.
4. Cross-fertilization: during the brainstorming, group members are likely to feed off and develop each other's responses.
5. Final discussion: allows synthesis and evaluation of ideas generated.

Structuring discussion using buzz groups
A buzz group comprises some two to four people discussing a question or a specific issue for a short period of time. It is a useful technique to focus the attention of each group member and allow each to contribute prior to a more general discussion. Discussion in buzz groups should be kept short. It may be appropriate for the complete group to form buzz groups several times during a group meeting, for example at the start of considering each new issue. It is also a useful technique when larger groups are in fixed rows of seats (eg, in a lecture theatre).

The following case study summarizes an approach to evaluating using listening and talking techniques.

The overall goal of the evaluation described here was to collect information from two cohorts of students as part of a course evaluation.

Initial meetings between the 'evaluator' (in this case a member of staff from outside the department responsible for the course) and course tutors were held to discuss factors such as:

— the aims of the evaluation
— constraints involved
— the audience for the findings
— practicalities, such as times when students could reasonably be contacted
— an overall plan for the evaluation, particularly for collecting information from students.

Information collected from students was to be used to inform discussion at the course committee about improvements and changes desirable, and also to form part of the overall yearly evaluation of the course.

Constraints which were taken into account included:

— limited time to undertake the collection of information
— a large number of students
— difficulty in assembling all the students in one place at one time.

As this was the first time such an evaluation had been undertaken for the particular course, it was considered that students should be given freedom to raise issues of personal importance, therefore initial phases of the process were open, with progressive focusing during later phases.

Information collected was to be synthesized into a written report to be discussed at the course committee: a mixture of staff responsible for teaching on the course and student representatives. The final plan is outlined below:

1. The evaluator met student representatives from each cohort separately. Meetings would best be described as 'informal non-structured discussions', the aim being for the evaluator to allow students the freedom of raising issues of relevance to them. The only prompting necessary to initiate discussion was an overview of the purposes of the evaluation followed by an open question, 'What do you think are the good and not so good aspects of your course?'.

   An hour's open discussion with each group of students led to the identification of a number of issues, summarized and synthesized by the evaluator at the end of discussion.

2. Issues identified during initial discussions formed the basis of a series of open questions on one side of A4 paper. Questions were checked for clarity and understanding by discussion with course tutors and a small sample of students.

3. A letter sent to each student on the course outlined the aims and organization of the evaluation, and prompted them to give some thought to the issues previously identified.

4. Students met in groups of approximately 30. These meetings were structured using snowballing, open questions forming the initial (individual) activity. After pairs had discussed the responses, groups of four were asked to identify any consensus of opinion about each of the issues. Such consensus was recorded on another (coloured) sheet of open questions.

   In this way a record of both individuals' and small-group responses was obtained for later analysis.

5. Each group of four was asked to feed back a comment to the whole group. Comments were recorded on acetate film so that the students could see them immediately and they could be easily taken away for later analysis.

6. Finally, open discussion was encouraged, once again the main points being recorded on acetate, using a pattern-type note. When a new issue was raised by the students, buzz groups were formed to focus initial thoughts.

Recording information from listening and talking

It is relatively easy to record information arising out of a highly structured interview where the respondent answers simple predefined questions. An open conversation is less easy to record. In terms of work and amount of time, structured techniques generally require more in the preparation stages whereas unstructured techniques require more during analysis.

When recording information, it is important to remember the ease with which data can be biased or distorted, often unconsciously. It is so easy to hear what one wants or expects to hear, or to forget the not so desirable points made. Objectivity can be aided by:

— having more than one person recording information
— discussing the recorded information with the respondents
— triangulation techniques (see page 66).

Note-taking

This is perhaps the most obvious technique for recording. Although practice and experience are vital, note-taking by one or more people present is applicable to a wide range of situations. If more than one person takes notes, later comparison is possible: we all have a tendency to hear what pleases us!

It may be possible to note only key words and phrases during the 'interview'. These could later be expanded, perhaps being given to those participating for their comment.

Some people find the patterned note used in the contents lists of this book an appropriate way of recording information, particularly in an unstructured situation where the same topic may be returned to several times.

In group discussions, it may be appropriate to make notes on overhead projector acetate, both allowing the group to see comments and also the group leader to take comments away easily.

Checklists

Pre-prepared checklists can be used during interviews and discussions. They provide a quick and easy way of recording information, while at the same time providing a series of reminders or prompts to the person organizing the session.

Checklists and notes may usefully be combined: checklists to record initial responses and comments and notes to record more detailed or open comments. (See page 64 for further details about checklists.)

Audio recording

Audio recording provides the possibility of giving a complete record of what was said during an interview or conversation. It may, however, inhibit some individuals and may raise more questions of confidentiality. Transcription of the tape also takes a great deal of time and is often a boring task.

It may be possible to record parts of discussions (say a summary) while using other techniques at other times. As always, care is needed to reduce the possibility of consciously or unconsciously biasing or distorting information. An extreme case known to the authors involved one person audio recording a committee meeting. When the 'transcript' was received it was noted by others present at the meeting to include only certain rather biased information. Needless to say, the full recording has been 'inadvertently' erased!

In addition to a valuable technique of recording information, audio recording is often useful to the organizer of the session in improving his or her skills.

Observation

Observing is something the majority of us spend much time doing. As was described earlier, teachers take notice of events while teaching, and may modify what they do in the light of what they see. A room full of puzzled faces and certain other forms of body language indicates to the teacher that further explanation is needed. Learners working in a small-group situation observe one another, make assumptions, and take decisions about specific roles, abilities, motivations, etc.

There are times when a more planned and systematic approach to observation may be necessary. Working within a particular environment for a period of time, the observer may become so familiar that he or she subconsciously becomes selective in what he or she sees. By making observation more systematic it is often easier to focus on particular aspects and to collect information pertinent to these. Observation is only one of a range of methods of collecting information. It may well be used in conjunction with other techniques; for example, observation combined with listening and talking is often a useful and powerful method of collecting information about what goes on inside 'classrooms'.

Styles of observation

Like all methods of collecting information, there is a spectrum of styles of observing, from the non-structured to the highly structured, from the observer being a participant in the activity being observed, to the observer being an 'outsider' or even a video camera. The style adopted will to an extent control the information collected. This is more likely to be a 'problem' with observation than with many other information-collecting techniques (see page 39 for further comment).

Non-structured (open) observation
Non-structured or 'open' observation, like non-structured inter-

views considered earlier, allows the collection of a rich variety of information. It is the technique of many social anthropologists. If the observer enters with as open a mind as possible, things may be seen and recorded which could be missed in a more structured or closed situation. However, practice and skill are needed by the observer in drawing on his or her experience and judgement to focus upon, and record, events considered to be important. It must be realized that however experienced the observer, only a fraction of the interactions and events occurring will be 'seen' and recorded. For this reason, it is often valuable to focus progressively upon certain aspects of particular interest.

Focusing could involve observing people in greater depth (eg, the teacher's interaction with a small group of learners, or the activities engaged by one learner or teacher over a period of time: tracking) or looking only for particular aspects of the learning situation (eg, the way the teacher organizes small-group activities). When focusing upon specific aspects, observation may continue to be open or some degree of structuring may be employed.

> As part of evaluating to help newly appointed teachers improve their teaching techniques, a colleague observes a series of sessions over a period of time. Although the broad aim is to help learners learn, initially no specific aspects are looked for.
>
> The observer watches a number of sessions with one group of learners, including formal lectures, group work and practicals. Field-notes are kept of things which seem interesting. After each observation, the two meet and discuss using the notes as prompts. It becomes clear that the organization of groups creates problems for the learners, and the observer progressively focuses upon this aspect. Groups are observed in turn and the observer starts to discuss with learners their feelings and problems. Information collected is used to discuss alternatives with the teacher who decides to try a range of different approaches. The observer (now focused upon the organization of group work and using listening and talking techniques in addition to observation) continues to report back to the teacher on apparent successes and failures of various styles of group work.

Structuring observation

By structuring observation it is possible to maintain focus upon particular aspects; also the job of observing and recording information may well be made easier. Very often (and particularly in the context of observing for the purposes of improving learning) observation will start in a non-structured way and, when issues of importance have been identified, some structuring will be valuable. Structuring can be employed at various levels, from the closed and pre-ordained categories of a commercially available observation schedule, through the observation schedule developed by the observer, to a simple checklist of items to look for and record.

In the context of this book, it is less likely that a highly structured closed observation schedule where specific behaviours are looked for and recorded at frequent intervals will be used. However, there may be some occasions when, for example, it is valuable to have accurate records of the types of questions asked by the learners or the amount of time the teacher spends interacting with the learners, giving instructions, asking questions, giving information, etc. In such cases, an observation schedule of the type shown on page 56 may be valuable.

A checklist is often a simple way of helping the observer structure his or her observation and record information. An example of a checklist designed to be used during observation of teaching/learning is shown below. It is intended to be used by an 'outside' observer, but could equally be used by the teacher or by one or more of the learners. In practice, greater space is left for written comments:

Aims of lesson
Environment
Use of student's previous knowledge
Organization of lesson
Pacing of lesson
Clarity of information
Use of aids
Attitude to learners
Learners' participation
Learners' feedback
Variety and level of questions:
— to learners
— from learners.

The headings allow the observer some flexibility while still maintaining focus. Comments written on the checklist form a useful starting point for discussions about the various aspects observed, between the observer, the teacher and it is to be hoped the learners. A principal aim here is that of improving understanding and increasing awareness about what happened during a lesson; the observer may well have as much to learn as the teacher!

I TEACHER TALK

Time in minutes

Ia *Teacher asks questions which are answered by:*

a_1 recalling facts and principles

a_2 applying facts and principles to problem-solving

a_3 making hypotheses or inferences from data

a_4 designing of experimental procedure

a_5 observation or interpretation of data

Ib *Teacher makes statements:*

b_1 of fact and principle

b_2 of problems

b_3 of hypothesis or speculation

b_4 of experimental procedure

b_5 of praise

b_6 of criticism

Ic *Teacher directs pupils to sources of information to:*

c_1 acquire or confirm facts or principles

c_2 identify or solve problems

c_3 make inferences, formulation or test hypotheses

c_4 seek guidance on experimental procedure

2 TALK AND ACTIVITY INITIATED AND/OR MAINTAINED BY PUPILS

2d *Pupils seek information or consult for the purpose of:*

d_1 acquiring or confirming facts or principles

d_2 identifying or solving problems

d_3 making inferences, formulating or testing hypotheses

d_4 seeking guidance on experimental procedure

2e *Pupils refer to teacher for the purpose of:*

e_1 acquiring or confirming facts or principles

e_2 seeking guidance when identifying or solving problems

e_3 seeking guidance when making inferences or testing hypotheses

e_4 seeking guidance on experimental procedure

	0	3	6	9	12	15	18	21	24	27	30
a_1											
a_2											
a_3											
a_4											
a_5											
b_1											
b_2											
b_3											
b_4											
b_5											
b_6											
c_1											
c_2											
c_3											
c_4											
d_1											
d_2											
d_3											
d_4											
e_1											
e_2											
e_3											
e_4											

The above observation schedule (adapted from *A Science Teaching Observation Schedule* by J Eggleston *et al.*) is designed to record talk by teachers and pupils. Each time talk which corresponds to a particular category is observed, a tick is placed in the appropriate box.

Recording information from observations

Information may be recorded by a variety of methods including:

— Field-notes
— Observation schedules or checklists
— Sound recording
— Video recording.

These could be used alone, or in combination.

Field-notes

Field-notes, either linear or patterned, allow the observer a great deal of freedom and latitude. What appears to be happening, together with comments or prompts for later discussion, can be recorded while observing. With practice, field-notes can be most effective, but it must always be remembered that no record will be absolute or objective however well intentioned or careful the writer. Analysis of field-notes can take time; one useful technique is to use a checklist of headings under which to summarize information.

Observation schedules or checklists

The types of schedules and checklists described earlier aid the recording and analysing of information and can form a useful starting point for later discussion. Even when using a pre-ordained checklist, it is still possible for the observer to make additional notes.

Audio and video recording

Audio and video recording can provide a comprehensive record of events as recorded through the microphone or camera lens. Unlike other techniques, they allow replay for observation, analysis and comment, perhaps by those who were earlier recorded and who may not be as prone to bias of information. However, the presence of audio or video equipment is likely to disturb the natural pattern of behaviour, and the camera or microphone will record only those events which they have been set up to monitor. For these reasons, care needs to be taken in their use and in the interpretation of recorded information. It is recommended that the advice of someone knowledgeable in audio and/or video techniques should be sought.

Audio recording can provide a complete record of verbal information and is therefore most appropriate where verbal interaction is the focus. It is often difficult to identify the various people recorded on tape; replaying the tape to the group may help. It may be necessary to use more than one microphone, and where much movement is involved, one or more radio-microphones may be necessary.

Video recording has the advantage of providing both audio and visual records and is a most powerful method of providing feedback to those recorded, perhaps being used to initiate group discussion (see page 46).

Pencil and paper techniques

There are many information-collecting techniques that involve the use of pencil and paper, ranging from casual notes to formal examinations. Below, we describe a range of such techniques aimed at collecting evaluative feedback from learners and teachers.

Like all evaluation tools, the techniques described here should be used as part of a planned exercise, and should be chosen paying due regard to purposes and alternatives. (See the introduction of this section for further details.)

Using assessments

Assessments can be used to provide valuable information about the learner's learning, the teacher's teaching and the resources used. All too often, both learners and teachers view assessment as an end point in learning and not as a means of facilitating or improving learning. As discussed throughout the book, we contend that assessment should be an integral and enabling part of the learning process. It should be of value to both learners and teachers in matching their needs.

Analysis of the results of assessments, by both learners and teachers, very often forms the starting point for looking in more detail at a particular problem or issue about learning. This can then be investigated further using techniques described elsewhere in this section.

The use of assessments as an evaluative tool is considered in more detail in Section 3 where it is discussed in terms of diagnosing learning and teaching.

Questionnaires

A questionnaire is a collection of written questions which are generally answered in the absence of the person who is collecting the information. Whereas most people would recognize that successful interviewing requires skill and experience, many consider that writing a questionnaire is an easy task. Unfortunately this is not so: it is all to easy to produce a questionnaire whose questions are ambiguous, instructions unclear, layout poor or information difficult to analyse later. As always, the purposes of using a questionnaire, and the likely uses of information collected, should be discussed and clarified.

Use of questionnaires

Questionnaires can collect information quickly from a large number of people, particularly when compared with one-to-one interviews. However, where information to be collected is complex, value laden or where in-depth probing of responses is required, questionnaires are of less applicability than listening and talking techniques.

It may be that a questionnaire is the only feasible way of collecting information in certain circumstances: for example, distance learning courses (but see Audioconferencing, page 166) where very large numbers are involved or where respondents wish to remain anonymous.

A questionnaire may well be used in conjunction with other information-collecting techniques. For example, one may be used at the start of snowballing (see page 47) or to collect information from a large number of learners after important issues have been identified during group meetings (see page 46).

Types of questions

Questions may be either open-ended or closed, allowing the respondent some latitude or very little.

		yes			no	
1.	Did you find the workshop useful?	[ ]			[ ]	
		very				not
2.	How useful did you find the workshop?	[ ]	[ ]	[ ]	[ ]	[ ]
3.	How useful did you find the workshop?	. . . .				
		. . . .				
		. . . .				

Questions 1 and 2 are examples of closed questions, whereas question 3 is more open-ended. Although basically asking the same question, the information received from the above is likely to be different for each question. An even more open question may be:

4. What were your reactions to the workshop?

Answers to question 4 are likely to display the most variation, depending upon:

— time made available
— space given on the questionnaire
— motivation of the person answering
— the number of respondents.

The choice between using open or closed questions depends upon what information is required, the audience, and the time available to write, answer and analyse the questionnaire.

Open-ended questions are quicker and easier to write than closed questions, but the resulting answers are more difficult and time-consuming to summarize. This may be an important consideration where large numbers are involved. Closed questions are often considered easy to answer, but many people become frustrated because they consider the choice of answers does not exactly fit their desired response.

Open-ended questions allow the respondents more freedom in the way they answer and in what information they give. For this reason they can collect information which would not be obtained with closed questions.

It may be advantageous to include both open and closed questions in the same questionnaire to allow people to expand answers and express opinions as well as providing specific information.

If closed questions are presented first, the people completing the questionnaire will have their attention drawn to certain points and this may affect their answers to the questions which follow. If open questions precede closed questions, the respondents are given freedom to express themselves before having their ideas focused by the questionnaire writer. A particularly useful combination for evaluation purposes is a closed question followed by an open one allowing the respondent to qualify his or her answer:

```
                                          very              not
5a. How useful did you find the workshop? [ ] [ ] [ ] [ ] [ ]
5b. How could it be made more useful for   . . . . . . . . . . . . . . . .
    you?                                   . . . . . . . . . . . . . . . .
                                           . . . . . . . . . . . . . . . .
```

Planning and developing a questionnaire
A questionnaire may be used alone, or may be one of several techniques used to collect information. However it is used, it needs to be planned and writing needs to be undertaken with

thought and care. Some initial questions to ask when planning to collect information are given on page 41. If it is decided to use a questionnaire, then the procedure for developing it may be:

1. Decide on the information needed, therefore on the content of the questionnaire.
2. Explore alternative types and sequences of question (eg, open, closed, use of different wording) and produce a first draft of the questionnaire.
3. Test the questions on a small sample, preferably people similar to those who will ultimately answer the questionnaire.
4. Redraft and edit in the light of the trials/pre-tests.

These stages could form the basis of a checklist as discussed on page 64.

When actually writing the questionnaire, remember that the aim is to obtain the information you want and that which the respondent wishes to give. The questionnaire should encourage those who are answering to do so easily and accurately. The following brief guidelines may help:

1. Questions and instructions should be easy to understand for the intended users, be kept as short as possible and be unambiguous.
2. Each question should deal with a single specific point.
3. Questions should not contain double negatives.
4. Questions and instructions should not show bias, lead the respondent towards a particular answer, or be objectionable in any way.
5. The sequencing of questions should help motivate the respondent (eg, start with questions that are easy to answer).
6. The layout of the questionnaire should be chosen to aid the respondent and should help later analysis (eg, do not cramp questions, keep a consistent layout, leave adequate space between questions and for answers).

Analysing and using information from questionnaires
The analysis of information given on questionnaires may consist of counting and tabulating numeric answers and summarizing open questions. If a computer is available this could be used, allowing quicker and possibly more sophisticated numerical analysis. Numerical information presented graphically is often a very useful form. (Programs which help with statistical analysis of information are available for use with many microcomputers.)

Information from questionnaires may be summarized and displayed on summary sheets or checklists. It is useful to consider the layout of these sheets when writing the questionnaire. For closed questions, it may be possible to use a blank questionnaire form as a summary sheet, noting by each question the overall answers to that question. For open questions, summary cards may be useful. Each time a new idea or comment is noted this is written on a card. If the same (or very similar) response is noted on another questionnaire, this is recorded by numbering the card corresponding to the comment. In this way, the set of cards summarizes responses and their frequency for each question.

Delphi technique

The Delphi method (named after the Delphi Oracle!) is a systematic way of collecting and combining ideas from a number of individuals. While encouraging a consensus of opinion, it also enables divergences from consensus to be identified and recorded. Briefly, the method involves collecting information which is later analysed and fed back to the members of the group to elicit new information, which is subsequently analysed and fed back. It therefore comprises a number of cycles of activity.

Initially used as a way of obtaining predictions from 'world experts', Delphi methods are often a valuable way of collecting evaluative information. However, due to the iterative nature of the technique, it is very time consuming for the organizer.

Those taking part do not need to come into contact. Information can be collected by questionnaire (see page 58) and fed back by short written reports (or use can be made of audioconferencing; see page 166). Alternatively, individual interviews may be used if appropriate.

A typical Delphi procedure could involve the following:

1. Information about a specific issue is collected from the group.
2. The organizer collates, analyses and summarizes this information. If, for example, a closed questionnaire has been used, then the summary may show numbers of responses to each item. If more open techniques have been used (eg, semi-structured interviews) the summary may be a short written report.
3. Information contained within the summary is fed back to the group for their consideration. This is likely to prompt a further set of comments.

    At this stage, participants are asked to consider their ideas

Figure 2.3

in light of the overall group response. In this way, individuals with only weak convictions may move towards the group norm, while those with strong feelings will justify their views.

4. Information generated from stage 3 is collected, and so the process continues as shown in Figure 2.3

Diaries

Diaries are written records of events noted from the perspective of the writer or writers. They can range from brief notes completed on a proforma or logsheet, to long and deeply insightful personal reports of events. Diaries are often most appropriate for building up a regular record of events over a period of time, such as events occurring within a group of students, or during the development of curriculum materials. They form a very useful method of monitoring learning during project-type work.

Year tutors in a large secondary school felt unable to teach satisfactorily due to frequent interruptions from students and other staff. As part of a larger evaluation intended to inform decisions about restructuring of the timetable, year tutors were asked to keep a simple diary over a period of four weeks, recording details of who consulted them, when, the time taken, the nature of the consultation and the priority they attached to the consultation. A proforma was designed for this purpose.

Analysis of the diaries indicated trends regarding the most busy times for tutors of each year group, the types of consultation at different times and the priority attached to different reasons for consultation. As a result, the school was able to restructure the year tutor's teaching to allow him or her free time when most needed, and to include specific times for the tutor to meet his or her year group for discussion, trouble shooting and to give administrative information. The latter was found to be a particularly valuable and efficient use of time by both students and staff, and formed the focus of a later evaluation.

During an audiovisual aids assignment, learners are asked to keep an accurate diary of events. This is intended to serve two main purposes:

1. It helps the learners to focus upon what they are doing, why they are doing it, and enables them to reflect on their successes and failures!
2. It provides a valuable record for the teacher during discussion with the learners, as much work is undertaken at a distance from the tutor.

PERSONAL DIARY

Date	Activity, problem, plan etc.	Location	Time spent	Material or equipment used

Checklists

Simple checklists are often a useful aid when collecting, recording and summarizing information. They are straightforward to write, easy to complete and help maintain focus. For example, the questions we noted on page 41 could form the basis of a checklist to be used by a group planning to evaluate. The first three questions are shown on page 65. Answers to each question can be completed either by individuals or by the group working together.

What do we hope to achieve?

How can important issues be identified?

Who shall be involved in evaluating?

When developing a technique of collecting information, a checklist could be used to check that each stage and aspect of the planning has been considered.

A group of teachers designed the checklist below to help them maintain focus during the development of a questionnaire. (The list given on page 61 was used as the basis of this checklist.)

1. The general area of interest.

2. Specific content areas.

3. The target group (age, any particular characteristics etc).

4. Is a questionnaire the most appropriate way of collecting information?
   (If 'no' then stop here!)

   yes [ ]

   no [ ]

5. The most appropriate format: open [ ]
                                                                   closed [ ]
                                                                    mixed [ ]

6. Types of closed question: yes-no [ ]
                                                                 checklist [ ]
                                                         multiple-choice [ ]
                                                                    rating [ ]

7. Later analysis of questionnaires considered?   [ ]

8. First draft completed?   [ ]

9. All draft questions and instructions evaluated by: peers [ ]
                                                         sample of
                                                     target group [ ]

10. All questions and instructions redrafted?   [ ]

11. Layout evaluated by: peers [ ]
                                                         sample of
                                                     target group [ ]

In addition, a further checklist was produced when evaluating the individual questions. This was based on the guidelines given on page 61.

Triangulation

Triangulation is the process of mapping out and explaining more fully. In an educational and training context the geographical analogy can be extended further. In order to map out part of the countryside, certain triangulation points have been established from which others are viewed in three directions. The approach of evaluation from different perspectives is the basis of triangulation. There are potentially five methods of triangulation, some of which are more common in education than others. The purpose of each is to reduce the distortion produced by evaluating in one context by one method. For example, using a structured questionnaire limits the responses that can be made to those questions which are asked. The questionnaire may be deliberately designed to elicit responses in a limited area determined by the originator. Because of the orginator's interest and the limitations of response, the questionnaire is filtering, biasing and distorting. Each method has a similar problem. If that questionnaire is used with one set of learners while their teacher is present, a further sampling bias will occur.

One obvious method of triangulation is to use three or more

different information-collecting techniques (eg, interviews, observations, questionnaires, group discussion). Ideas which occur from two or more techniques have more reliability than those from only one. However, if the interview and questionnaire are both structured in a similar way, similar responses are to be expected! An alternative is to use the same techniques on different occasions which checks for consistency of the respondent's view over time.

Another method is to use three or more different investigators or observers. The sharing of perspectives, data and information enables the clarification of interpretations and a critical review of techniques. This sharing and critical reviewing also enables the involvement of learners and teachers in the process, ie, using evaluation to facilitate learning.

An interesting form of triangulation is called time triangulation. Many techniques give a snapshot at one point in time (eg, a questionnaire or an examination). An alternative approach is to track an individual learner over a period of time (a sort of 'cine' approach). A mixture of the cross-sectional (snapshot) and longitudinal (cine) approaches again aids confidence in data and information.

The remaining three methods are more difficult to explain in the context of a small-scale self-evaluation.

1. *Space triangulation* involves cross-cultural or cross sub-cultural investigations. This method can be very illuminating with respect to formal procedures, such as structured questionnaires, attitude scales and so on, where different cultures may interpret the words and their intention differently (this is particularly so for attitude scales which can be very culturally biased).
2. *Levels triangulation* involves using different individuals, groups or collectivities (eg, organizations, societies, cultures). While the variation in techniques suggested earlier may enable this, here the design of the evaluation would specifically aim at this form of triangulation.
3. *Theoretical triangulation* involves different investigators using different or competing theories. One way of presenting this type of triangulation is by using advocates for each theory, presenting their case as in a court of law.

While evaluating can be systematic it cannot be compared with a scientific investigation. In science if there are 32 variables, 29 may be kept constant while the remaining three are investigated.

A single method can be chosen which will give unambiguous information on these selected phenomena. Human interactions are complex and multi-variate. The techniques used to investigate the interactions are not neutral — they filter and give a selective experience of the environment. When one technique biases and distorts the picture, the data can be an artefact of the technique or of the collector of information. The multi-technique approach will give more confidence, especially if contrasting techniques are used.

> A college wished to investigate the attitudes of its day-release students to their time in college. The immediate suggestion was an attitude scale to be developed specifically for the purpose. The technique would be convenient to use, provide data in a quantitative form and be easily accessible to critics and employers. However, many attitude scales have little or no psychological bases or criteria for design. The scale will probably be culture-bound, so ethnic minorities and different socio-economic status groups will give different responses. It will probably get different responses on different occasions: so it is time-bound. Alternative approaches considered were an in-depth study of individuals over a period of time. Because the study is of individuals, it is idiosyncratic while providing insights. In addition such studies are difficult to replicate. Alternative approaches based on these techniques chosen were:
>
> — track individuals and identify key issues as a basis for a questionnaire for all students
> — use a questionnaire and track in depth a sample (for example, very positive, very negative, ethnic minority, high performer, low performer).
>
> Both of these are using time and method triangulation.

Large-scale evaluations may be able to use multi-methods (eg, teachers' ratings of learners, records of achievement, psychometric data, sociometric data, case studies, observation) and repeat these in several representative organizations.

It should be clear that objective 'scientific' approaches (eg, normative assessment procedures) give more generalized information and less idiosyncratic information, while subjective individualized approaches (eg, tracking, case studies) give more idiosyncratic information and less generalized information.

One monitoring system sometimes used with qualitative data is a panel of judges. Is it a form of triangulation if all the judges on the panel subscribe to the same values? Critics liken the panel of judges to a mystery tour. The passengers on one mystery tour had a sweepstake as to their destination; the driver won $48!

A possible routine for an evaluation procedure incorporating triangulation could be:

1. Identify area of interest/problem; it may be helpful to specify purposes in detail; it will certainly be necessary to reduce the scope to something which is manageable; identify expected reporting method.
2. Identify setting, administrative and organizational structures, procedural problems, finance and resources available.
3. Identify potential techniques; list possibilities and relate to information required; determine from total picture whether methods are efficient, supportive or unsuitable; identify which are quantifiable and non-quantitative, which use individual responses, and which use group responses; determine which techniques are going to be considered most important.
4. Make decisions on the extent and range of information which will meet the original criteria to provide a balanced (triangulation) framework within the resources available.
5. Implement the decisions; devising piloting techniques then collecting and analysing data.
6. Interpret the data to give information in a suitable form for reporting.

The triangulation has been built into this process, but it is important to identify the form(s) of triangulation used.

Suggested group activities

1. *How do we identify issues of real importance?*
Ask the group either to brainstorm or to use a snowball technique. Alternatively, one member of the group could be asked to describe what led to evaluating in an instance with which he or she is familiar.

2. *How can an evaluation be planned and techniques chosen?*
What we are about is developing a plan, or strategy for evaluating. We have found a case study approach to be particularly valuable. The case study could be given to the group, or a real example could be used with which one or more of the group is familiar. The whole group could be split into smaller groups (say four or six members) who work from guidelines indicating specific tasks. For example, with school teachers the case study may be:

The geography department, which is part of the humanities sector (comprising careers, economics, geography, history, religious education and social studies departments), introduced a new series of study packs used for about half of the year, by their fourth-year mixed ability students.

After examination at the end of the year, teachers have begun to express disquiet over the apparent progress of their students. Initial reaction to the packs which are well illustrated and attractively presented had been favourable. However, it is now being questioned whether or not the new material is providing an effective learning resource.

The group could be asked to read through the first part of Section 2 (pages 35–42) and discuss the list of questions on page 41, and draw up a checklist of answers to these. Any group finishing the process early could be asked to start considering techniques in more detail. When all groups have finished, they give a brief report to the whole. The groups may like also to evaluate how well they functioned as a group.

3. *Developing techniques and instruments for collecting information*
Once again, small groups (say four to six members) working together generally function more successfully than a large group. This activity could follow from (2) above, or could be separate. If one or more of the group has a real need, so much the better. We have found several approaches which work well:

— Developing a technique or instrument for a particular purpose (eg, a group discussion to collect particular information). It may be useful to use a checklist to help maintain focus and provide the group with prompts.
— The analysis of 'specimen' instruments (eg, several question-naires could be provided for the group to discuss, evaluate and rewrite).
— The use of a case study or situation.

If several groups are working, then different groups could use different approaches, reporting and discussing differences later.

The relevant parts of this section could be used to provide prompts to the group.

4. *What is the utility of evaluating?*
Use one of the group discussion techniques noted in this section.

5. *Who evaluates the evaluators?*
A discussion based around this question will raise many funda-
mental issues, including those of a philosophical and sociological
nature.

Difficulties and criticisms

The evaluating that we have described depends heavily on
qualitative and indirect methods. The data and information is
collected in a semi-structured or non-structured way. The
analysis of the data and information is done by an individual or
a group. The process of filtering, analysing and reporting is not
explicit, whereas structured approaches make more explicit the
filtering and bias by the very questions which are used. The more
qualitative approaches are open to distortion, making them less
reliable and open to questions of validity. The suggestion of continuous communication with those involved in the course helps to
overcome these problems.

The qualitative style of evaluating enables the writing of reports
which are easy and interesting to read or hear, particularly where
quotations are included from actual participants. However, selection of which quotations to use and the ordering of the report are
very much in the creative hands of the presenter. That presenter
will have personal values (or even axes to grind) and, however
honest, will tend to bias the report to support his or her own
values. One way of overcoming this problem is for the presenter
to start by giving his or her own views or values so that the report
can be judged taking these into account. Again the offering of a
draft report for critical review by those involved can provide an
opportunity for editing or the incorporation of different views. On
several major projects in the USA there has been a review of the
evidence by a different set of workers who also bring together
their conclusions. These conclusions may conflict with those of the
original workers. The alternative reports have been published
incorporating a discussion between the two sets of workers. This
strategy has potential but is obviously time consuming. Another
strategy is to use different advocates who present their cases based
on the evidence, rather like a court of law.

The reporting often provides the sort of information that is
useful to local authorities, funding bodies and employers in order
to make judgements. Much current evaluating in institutionalized
education and training has moved towards internal institutional
evaluating using more qualitative and illuminative styles. It is

71

easier to doctor the report to give a rosy picture than it would be with conventional quantitative data. However, the use of the report as a means of judging the evaluating process is a 'tail wagging the dog' problem. The advantage of the process is the learning which takes place.

If we focus on the learning process for the institution or the learning system, a rather different picture emerges. The responsibility for part of the evaluating can be with the learner, and part can be done co-operatively between teachers and learners. The focus of the process is about improving the potential for learning. The collecting and analysing of data will probably encourage communication which did not occur before. By communicating during the spiral process (see page 38) the learning environment will be changed. Here, the evaluating is not about ensuring that no change takes place before the report is presented, but about enabling innovation and change as a collaborative venture of all those involved.

Where evaluating is focused around the objectives or criteria of the course, there are potential difficulties. It is always possible to carry out fine tuning of a course to ensure that criteria are met better and better. However this inward-looking approach fails to consider two other important aspects. The criteria may need challenging; who decided on those criteria, and why are they relevant in the particular context under review? What other learning is occuring that is not specified by the criteria?

A potential source of information, which was only briefly mentioned, is learners who have already completed the course. A representative sample may be difficult to locate. The relevance of criteria may be a case where learners now in the next stage of their development (whether still learning or in real-life situations) will have firm views. The potential for using past learners in association with current learners is considerable if evaluating is seen as a learning process.

Some will see the evaluating as not going far enough along the lines of improving practice by enabling teachers and learners to elicit and modify one another's value systems. These processes require, for example, video recordings of actual learning sessions where teacher and learners explain what they think was happening. The approach can be very threatening to all concerned so should only be used where all parties are in agreement and experienced and sensitive 'evaluators' are involved. It is clearly easier to use where face-to-face contact occurs rather than distance study.

Finally a further criticism can be made that the assumptions behind a highly structured imposed evaluation such as that used by the first evaluator on the buses is incompatible with an unstructured facilitator (a participant observer such as the fourth evaluator). In our opinion this is not always so; the strategies and styles of evaluating should relate to the problem being investigated rather than being ordered by philosophical dogmatism.

Annotated bibliography

Bloom, B S, Madaus, G F and Hastings, J T (1981)
Evaluation to Improve Learning
New York: McGraw Hill.

The book is about the state of the art for assessing students' learning. It is aimed at classroom teachers, with a focus on the improvement of students' learning. There are sections covering issues such as: objectives; learning for mastery; summative, diagnostic and formative assessment; writing and selecting items for various levels of cognitive learning.

Delbecq, A L, Van de Ven, A H and Gustafson, D H (1975)
Group Techniques for Program Planning
Illinois: Scott, Forsman.

Describes in detail the theory and application of the Delphi and nominal group techniques.

Eggleston, J, Galton, M and Jones, M (1976)
Processes and Products of Science Teaching
London: Macmillan.

Hamilton, D *et al.* (eds) (1977)
Beyond the Numbers Game
London: Macmillan.

An extremely readable collection of papers on evaluation. Contains a wide range of extracts from most of the eminent evaluators, the central thesis being that evaluation involves far more than measurement of outcomes.

Harlen, W (ed) (1978)
Evaluation and the Teacher's Role
Basingstoke: Macmillan.

A collection of papers dealing with a wide range of evaluation issues; many have a focus on 'evaluation for innovation'.

Harris, N D C, Bell, C D and Carter, J E H (1981)
Signposts for Evaluating: a Resource Pack
London: Council for Educational Technology/Schools Council.

A pack providing basic materials for teachers involved in institutional or classroom evaluation. The pack is in three parts: an introduction to evaluating; techniques for evaluating; and some theoretical aspects of evaluating. The techniques elaborated vary from assessment procedures to curriculum analysis, and from observation to interviewing.

Harrison, C (1980)
Readability in the Classroom
Cambridge: Cambridge University Press.

A practical guide for teachers for assessing readability and matching notes and books to learners. Specific reference is made to the problems found in various subjects. The main readability formulas are described and assessed, and there is comment on how they can be used when writing material. The book also includes a computer program for assessing readability.

Hartley, J (ed) (1980)
The Psychology of Written Communication
London: Kogan Page.

A collection of articles addressing issues such as: theoretical aspects of learning; how learners develop writing skills; how to design written information so as to have maximum impact; the use of microfilm, viewdata and computer systems; scientific writing. There is a useful section on the design of written information.

Huczynski, A (1983)
Encyclopaedia of Management Development Methods
Aldershot: Gower.

Although the title is indicative of a specific audience, it is likely that all educators and trainers will find much of relevance in this book. Some 300 methods of providing learning/teaching situations are outlined, generally with references to sources of more detailed information. In addition, a framework is provided to help teachers choose and analyse methods.

Kaufman, R and English, F W (1979)
Needs Assessment: Concept and Application
Englewood Cliffs, New Jersey: Educational Technology Publications.

The book is divided into two sections: concepts and basic models underlying needs assessment to provide a framework for successful application; applications of the most useful models including case studies of needs assessment in education, government, commerce, industry and the armed services.

Payne, S L (1951)
The Art of Asking Questions
Princeton: Princeton University Press.

Although now an old text, this is still a useful source of information about the importance of the ways in which questions are asked. Many practical hints and tips are given through the frequent use of examples.

Rowan, J and Reason, P (1981)
Human Inquiry: A Source Book of New Paradigm Research
London: Wiley.

Shipman, M (1979)
In-School Evaluation
London: Heinemann.

Aims to provide a 'do-it-yourself' manual for evaluating a wide range of curricular and extra-curricular activities. These are also applicable outside the school environment. The book describes in plain language various assessment techniques, both internal and external.

Shrock, S A (1984)
Naturalistic Inquiry: an Alternative Methodology for Instructional Development Research.
In Bass, R K and Dills, C R (eds) *Instructional Development: The State of the Art II*
Dubuque, Iowa: Kendall/Hunt.

The paper considers non-obtrusive means of inquiry while dealing with colleagues and clients, rather than the more traditional experimental design using obtrusive methods.

Strachan, R M (ed) (1983)
Guide to Evaluating Methods: A Manual for Microtechnology Innovation
Cambridge: National Extension College.

Although the focus in case studies is on microelectronics innovation, the majority of the text has wider applicability. A brief outline of a wide range of evaluation techniques is given. These are discussed in the context of improvement of curriculum materials and of learning.

Straughan, R and Wrigley, J (eds) (1980)
Values and Evaluation in Education
London: Harper and Row.

An interesting examination of standards, measurements, assessment, evaluation and values in education. The links between these concepts are explored in depth. The second part of the book looks at the ways in which these concepts arise in different subject areas of the curriculum.

Stubbs, M and Delamont, S (1976)
Explorations in Classroom Observation
Chichester: John Wiley.

Focuses on the study of what happens between learners and teachers, describing (often via case study) methods of observing, recording and analysing interactions. Provides a brief but valuable overview of research into teaching/learning.

Wragg, E C (1979)
Designing and Analysing Interviews
Nottingham University Rediguide II
Maidenhead: TRC Rediguides.

This is a small book which describes uses and different styles of interviews, and some of the pitfalls of interviewing. It is a good starting point for anyone needing straightforward information.

Section 3 Assessing for Learning

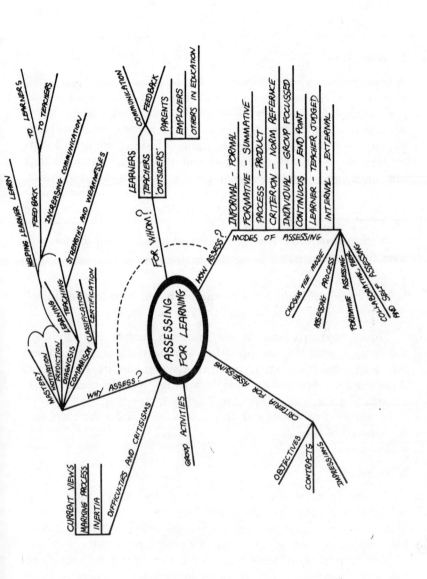

3. Assessing for Learning

Introduction

Assessing of sorts has been with us from the beginning of recorded history. The Romans used many different types of assessing, and earlier there was Eve with the apple! All indications are that it will remain with us for the foreseeable future at most levels of compulsory and post-compulsory education. Indeed, we are all continually assessing and passing judgement on fellow human beings and inanimate objects. Judgements are based on our own value systems and those prevalent in society. In some situations assessing is made by an 'expert' judge or critic: the art critic, the music critic, the external examiner.

In education and training, two broad aspects form the focus of assessing:

1. the learners, and
2. the 'resources' which are assembled to aid learning, including print, media, curricula and the teachers themselves.

Throughout this book we use the term 'assessing' to indicate the former, and 'evaluating' when we are discussing the latter. Although this distinction is commonly made in Britain, in American literature the word 'assessing' is little used in this context, 'evaluating' serving to label both concepts.

In the first part of this section we broadly consider the why? and for whom? of assessing.

Why assess?

Try thinking of reasons why assessing often takes such a key position in education. Or better, try to persuade colleagues and/or learners to do the same. (See the activities at the end of this section for one way of organizing such an activity.)

There are many reasons suggested for keeping clear records of learners' progress, for example to help the learner realize what he or she has learned, to help the teacher plan for future learning or remediation. These records originate from some form of informal or formal assessing organized either by the teacher or by the learner. The recording and discussion of assessing often forms the basis of the main communication between the teacher and the learner. Assessing without communication is of doubtful value: communication between the teacher and the learner is an essential part of the learning process and should be on a regular basis. An obvious problem is that the means of communication may well need to be different for different learners according to their character and preferred styles of learning. The relative roles of teacher and learner are also crucial: in schools where the teacher is more mature, it is easy to become patronizing; in higher and adult education the learner may be more mature. If the communication between teacher and learner is to have any meaning in a motivational or learning context, its aims need to be clear and it needs to be carefully planned and executed. (Some ways of facilitating and evaluating communication are discussed in Section 2.)

Another important aspect of the communication is the accessibility of the teacher to the learner. In distance study, for example, the only means of communication between the learner and the teacher may be by telephone or mail. It is clear that the style and method of communication and of assessing will be very different in this situation from that where the teacher and the learner have access at any hour of the day, such as in a residential learning environment.

In formal institutionalized education and training, the contact between learner and teacher can be worse than in distance study. For example, if the learning is mainly focused around lectures, the teachers may carry such a high load of lectures that no other contact is available to the learners. Although it would be hoped that such an extreme case did not exist, nevertheless the higher the workload for both teachers and learners, the less likely it is that communication and regular assessing will occur.

When the focus is on small-group work, there is no guarantee that there is any better communication and contact, although where the small-group work is centred around the development of interpersonal skills it is more likely to occur. The normal way to help communication develop is to allocate personal tutor time for each learner; however, this can be counter-productive as the responsibility for the learning is once again being vested in the teacher rather than in the learner. In the long term, each of us needs to take more and more responsibility for our learning in a world where the knowledge base alone is increasing at a phenomenal rate, let alone the technological developments which give us all more access to information and more difficulty in discriminating between that which is relevant and useful and that which is garbage! Similarly the role of the teacher changes to a guide, facilitator or even a co-traveller rather than a presenter or performer. We return to this in Sections 4 and 5.

In the following pages we examine some of the reasons most commonly advocated for assessing learners:

— increasing the motivation of learners
— prediction of an individual's potential
— diagnosis of learning
— diagnosis of teaching
— certification, classification and comparison with other learners.

It must not be overlooked that, as a part of education, assessing is to a lesser or greater extent a tool of socialization into a particular society, a political activity which may well be aimed at perpetuating certain values, encouraging change, or maintaining the status quo.

Assessing for mastery

There are many aspects of learning which require mastery on behalf of the learner. The pharmacist mixing drugs would be short-lived in his or her profession if correct quantities were obtained only 85 per cent of the time. The trainee mechanic replacing the parts of an engine would be most unpopular if only three-quarters of the parts were correctly assembled! In these cases, assessing is both a valuable and necessary part of the learning process, providing feedback to both the learner and teacher. In general, interest will be on the learner's ability to achieve the desired result (a correctly mixed drug or an engine which works) rather than upon comparing one learner with another.

In the examples used above, the focus of assessing is on the mastery or non-mastery of specific skills. It is likely that importance is attached to such mastery and, if a particular learner takes longer than average to achieve it, this will be considered acceptable. The tendency is towards 'fixed learning, variable time' rather than the more normally found 'fixed time, variable learning'.

Assessing for motivation

Assessing may increase the motivation of the learner. However, it has other more negative effects such as increasing stress or decreasing the desire to continue studying. The dividing line between motivation and demotivation is a fine and varying one. It is likely to be different for each learner and for a particular learner it will vary from time to time. These factors must be borne in mind by those organizing the assessing, and by the learners themselves.

The motivational effects of assessing may well be due to different factors, for example the effects of:

— knowing that one is to be assessed
— knowing, or anticipating, the results of assessing
— being involved in the process of assessing.

It would be encouraging to think that these factors go towards increasing the motivation of learners in their learning. But, equally, the learner who constantly gets low marks could be discouraged from trying. The assignment out of class, the driving test, and the end of unit examination are likely to act as carrots, or big sticks, depending upon the individual's point of view, the way in which assessing is presented and the actual processes adopted. There is a large difference between the 'motivational' effects due to knowing that one is to be assessed and those due to helpful and constructive feedback about some work.

Throughout the book, we concentrate upon the motivational aspects of assessing and evaluating and discuss ways of using these in order to facilitate learners' learning.

Assessing for prediction

Although only a limited number of assessment tools and techniques are designed with prediction as their aim, many are used in this way. In secondary/high schools, class examinations often form the basis to judge future courses of study. Examinations at 16 + are used to select those learners considered 'suitable' for entry to further courses. Examination results are used as an important factor for selection to employment and particularly to higher education.

Likewise, in higher education, assessing often forms hurdles over which learners have to jump in order to continue with their chosen course of study or to obtain specific qualifications or credits for employment. In much of technical and commercial training, success at one level opens the possibility of training at a higher level.

In all of these cases, if it is assumed that 'those who score well now will score well later', then assessing is probably being used as a predictor of future potential. Although often used in this way, many studies have shown that frequently used assessments have little predictive value of an individual's future performance. Even the results of examinations used to select for higher education in a similar subject area rarely indicate a high degree of correlation with final degree results. A higher correlation may well be found between the learner's motivation, and/or style of learning, rather than between traditionally used predictors.

Assessing for diagnosis of learning

Assessing has an important role to play in the diagnosis of learning (that is the identification of learning that has apparently taken place, learning difficulties experienced by individuals or groups, or identification of future learning needs). Used in this way, assessing does not necessarily involve formal tests or measurements and is unlikely to involve comparative grading of learners. Here, we are not discussing diagnostic assessment instruments used by specialists to diagnose particular learning difficulties, but more usual assessments used by teachers and learners in a diagnostic way, focusing upon either individuals or groups. The latter has much relevance to the diagnosis of possible teaching (or organizational problems) as noted below.

During teaching, teachers constantly attempt to assess learning, from asking direct questions to receiving non-verbal communication from learners. Likewise, the learners are likely to be constantly assessing themselves, their peers, the environment and their teacher. All help to inform the learners and teacher of their successes and failures in achieving goals, and it is to be hoped, aid 'fine tuning' or 'hole patching and plugging'. In this area the activities of 'assessing' and 'evaluating' tend to blur into each other. The major aim of assessing used in a diagnostic way is to provide information of use in helping learners to learn, the recurrent theme of this book. In order to identify difficulties a crucial element is discussion between learners themselves and between learners and teachers, based on the assessing.

Assessing for diagnosis of teaching

In the previous section we have briefly considered assessing as being focused upon the learning achieved by learners. However, assessing learners may well provide valuable information about the teaching, organization or curriculum to which learners have been subjected. Consider a simple example where learners have answered a number of assessment items producing the simplified results shown in Figure 3.1. The items could be formal test questions, project marks or even peer assessing. For simplicity, we have shown numeric 'marks'. Comments, informal assessing and the results of questionnaires could well form the basis for this application.

The results may be treated in a number of ways. For comparison of learners, it is most probable that the total marks of each learner would be compared. However, in the above example the total marks for assessment B are lower than totals for other questions. Is this due to:

1. Problems with the assessing itself?
2. Lower than average quality of teaching in the area of work to which the assessing relates?
3. The majority of learners failing to have studied the work to which the assessing relates?
4. Work inappropriate to the learners involved?
5. Lack of confidence among the learners?
6. A different standard of marking for the assessment?

Assessment Learner	A	B	C	D	E	Total
Alison	8	4	7	5	9	33
Brian	4	3	7	5	8	27
Chris	2	4	6	5	7	24
Duncan	8	2	5	4	5	24
Elisa	4	1	4	7	6	22
Total	26	15	29	26	35	

Figure 3.1

Without further analysis, only a guess could be made, but considered in this way the results of assessing could well lead to a questioning of teaching methods or the appropriateness of the curriculum content. It may form the starting point of more detailed evaluating aimed at improving learning. (Evaluating is considered further in Section 2.)

Assessing for certification, classification and comparison

We have chosen to group together certification, classification and comparison not because they must be inextricably related, but because in practice the dividing lines are often very blurred.

It can be argued that much assessing currently practised in education has certification, classification or comparison as one of its major aims. The learner is tested in relation to other learners and to the values ascribed by society. Results of such assessing are used to rank and select, allowing employers and the education system to choose.

In this book, we do not concentrate upon these purposes of assessing. Those wishing further details are referred to the bibliography at the end of this section.

Assessing for whom?

There are inextricable relationships between the purposes of assessing and their intended audiences. Taking an extreme example, it would be of little use to use an assessment tool intended to highlight teaching difficulties, in order to provide information of value to a future employer about the achievements of an individual applicant. However, there are many instances where assessing can have a variety of purposes, for example it may be used to provide information to the learner about strengths and weaknesses, while at the same time providing information to the teacher of a 'hole plugging and patching' nature.

In earlier parts of the text we have suggested that possible audiences for the 'results' of assessing are the learners, the teachers, and other 'outsiders' (eg, potential employers, teachers in other institutions).

Assessing for the learners

Rarely is assessing organized with the learners as the main audience for the results, yet if assessing is to be a real aid to learners' learning they must be an important audience whatever the purpose, mode or technique of assessing.

For assessing to be of maximum use to learners, the learners need to be involved in the assessment process. This must include active involvement in feedback, and may well include involvement with the design and judgement of assessing. The latter is inherent in collaborative assessing discussed on page 102. In distance learning, 'involvement' in feedback may have to be limited to writing to, or at best telephoning or audioconferencing (see the Appendix) with the teacher and other learners. In a face-to-face situation it can involve more, from simple questions and answers about marked assessment to full negotiation of judgements.

Case studies presented later in this section, and at various parts throughout the book, indicate some of the ways in which communication between learner and teacher about assessments can be organized. It is not the method which is important, but the aims and processes of providing feedback. Many of the approaches more usually associated with evaluating are applicable.

Assessing for the teachers

Both formal and informal assessing have applications for the teacher involved in learning. They provide feedback to the teacher about the effectiveness of his or her teaching (or of his or her facilitation of learning) as we have previously indicated. In this way the results of assessing may be an aid to evaluating the course. In practice it is often a feeling that 'something is wrong with the results' which raises issues and forms the starting point of the spiral of evaluating introduced on page 38. Feedback which allows the teacher to make informed judgements about the learners is also provided, perhaps for purposes of diagnosis and remediation, planning further teaching, report and reference writing, selection or prediction.

Results of assessing, whether they be marks in a mark book, informal impressions or detailed comments arrived at during collaborative assessing, are there to be used to help the learners, not just to be kept in a file.

Assessing for 'outsiders'

In the present context, by 'outsiders' we mean those not directly involved in the learning/teaching process being assessed. These may include parents, potential employers, teachers in other organizations and institutions and administrators. In certain circumstances they may include those undertaking educational research or perhaps educational psychologists using diagnostic instruments. Although this audience may be less important in the context of assessing for learning, it is often all important to individual learners. An external public examination may well hold the key to college entrance or employment. A profile report may be used by employers to determine job progression. Often, assessing designed with 'outsiders' as the main audience provides very little feedback to either learner or teacher about an individual's strengths and weaknesses. A grade C or 3 in a public examination does not help the learner plan for future learning (although it may well bar the way for certain learning) nor does it provide much information of use to the teacher to help him or her come to know the learner's own strengths and weaknesses in the learning the teacher has organized. In addition, assessing used in this way as a predictor of some sort may be inappropriate as we have noted previously.

More positively, results of assessing can provide useful information to 'outsiders' if reported with the aim of aiding learning. For example, parents are important in helping their children learn. Greater positive contact between institutionalized and everyday educators can help learners learn. Diagnosis of problems, strengths and weaknesses as a result of assessing can be used by parents. It cannot be used unless it is communicated and discussed in a meaningful way.

Communication between different teachers who teach a particular learner, or from one teacher to the next who will be responsible, should be used to provide continuity and facilitate learning. How often do teachers in an institution or organization have meaningful communication about individual learners' strengths, weaknesses and needs, let alone pass on relevant and helpful information to teachers in the learners' future institutions? How often is much time spent 'diagnosing needs' or 'bringing the group up to the required level' when the relevant information could so easily be made available?

How can we assess?

We believe that decisions relating to assessing can make or break a learning situation. We must emphasize that assessing is not only the conventional marking of written work but also includes many other aspects: project or syndicate work, informal feedback (see Section 2), self- and peer assessing. It is these 'alternatives' which can be focused upon aiding learners to learn that we concentrate on in this section and elsewhere in the book.

Learners need not have all their achievements recorded but the learners and the teachers need to see progress throughout the course of learning. Any documentation arising must be that which can be defended to, understood and accepted by all those involved: learners, teachers, other organizations and institutions, possible employers. The whole process should be focused on active involvement by the learner in his or her learning. It is not the actual methods or tools of assessing which we believe should be changed in many cases, rather the aims and ethos of their use and application.

There is a vast range of types of assessing available. From informal and casual observations, through teacher-organized and marked questions, standardized tests, to assessment criteria devised and used by the learners themselves. All have a place in facilitating learning, but not all may be realistic or desirable in any particular situation. Like all learning/teaching activities, assessing needs to be carefully chosen to suit the intended purposes, expected outcomes and constraints. We do not provide details of specific assessment instruments, but concentrate on highlighting issues which we believe are relevant to the theme of the book: how assessing can be used to facilitate and improve learning. A wide range of instruments can be used, for example comprehension exercises, diagnostic tests, diaries, essay assignments, individual or group discussion, mini research projects, multiple-choice, open book tests, oral tests, practical projects, problem solving, profile recording, self-assessment questions and questionnaires. It is why and how they are used which are important. Those readers who require details of particular instruments are directed to the bibliography at the end of this section.

When deciding upon assessment techniques, an appropriate starting point is to consider two questions:

1. What are the overall purposes, or aims, of assessing?
2. Who is the audience for the results of assessing?

These questions have been specifically considered in the previous parts of this section and are recurrent throughout the book. When the aims and audiences of assessing have been discussed and clarified (see the group activities at the end of this section) it is valuable to consider a number of factors or 'modes' relating to assessing before developing the actual technique.

Modes of assessing

Let us consider eight modes of assessing which we have listed as bipolar constructs:

1. Informal — formal
2. Formative — summative
3. Process — product
4. Criterion-referenced — norm-referenced
5. Individual-focused — group-focused
6. Continuous — end-point
7. Learner-judged — teacher-judged
8. Internal — external.

The constructs should not be seen as being absolute or mutually exclusive. For example, it is possible to use a particular assessment both formatively *and* summatively, at the same time assessing both elements of process *and* of product. Likewise, the constructs 'continuous — terminal' and 'course work — examinations' are in most cases likely to have a close relationship with each other. Nevertheless, consideration of these constructs forms a valuable way of discussing factors involved in the choice of an assessment technique or in the analysis of a technique already in use. (The activities at the end of this section give some ideas about discussing the aspects noted above.)

We briefly discuss each of these constructs in turn. Some of the aspects which we consider to be more relevant to assessing for learning are subsequently expanded.

Informal–formal

Informal assessing in education, as in all walks of life, is an inevitable and ongoing phenomenon which is often carried out unconsciously. Teachers observe learners, learners observe teachers, both observe learning aids; judgements are made. Formal assessing is more of a planned and obtrusive activity. Time is set aside, learners generally realize that they are being assessed, and results are said to have a particular purpose which is usually known by both learners and teachers.

Informal assessing plays a very important part in education, often much more difficult to qualify or quantify than that of more formal assessing. Although both teachers and learners are continually assessing events informally, in most institutionalized education the balance of power is towards the teacher. Much information used by teachers is the result of informal assessing: report writing, references, discussion with colleagues, discussion with learners. Negatively, it can be argued that informal assessing is usually subjective, often undertaken covertly and may be the result of personal preferences and dogma. However, it can equally be argued that the majority of informal assessing by teachers is (or at least should be) exercised with the aim of helping learners and teachers become more aware of themselves; their strengths, weaknesses and future needs.

As teachers assess learners informally, the reverse is also constantly happening. Learners' assessments of their teachers have important effects on learning and on the general milieu of the learning environment. Individuals' attitudes towards learning are affected by how the organizers of learning are viewed. Indeed (and unfortunately) learners are sometimes described as jellies who tend to mould and model themselves on their teachers: a motivated teacher leads to a motivated group of learners; a demotivated or lax teacher leads to less than optimum attitudes towards learning. This is as true of adult learners as it is of those in primary schools.

Assessing for learning must involve teachers and learners sharing their informal assessments and judgements, becoming more open and helping each other identify needs, possibilities, strengths and weaknesses. This is a key focus of other sections of the book. Section 2 in particular introduces methods of helping people communicate and share ideas.

Formative – summative

The terms 'formative' and 'summative' which are often used in the context of evaluation can equally be applied to the intentions of assessing learners. Formative assessing is about using the process and results of assessing to influence and, it is to be hoped, to facilitate the learning process. Summative assessing is focused more on using results for some external reason, perhaps for deciding whether or not a particular learner should be allowed to continue with a course of study. It may come at the end of a particular learning experience with which the learner will not be continuing. The distinction is blurred; a terminal test may help the learner realize his or her strengths and weaknesses and modify learning (or teaching). However, we wonder if it is reasonable to consider an external public examination as having much of a formative role, other than in preventing certain learners from doing certain things or obtaining certain positions.

To facilitate learning we believe that assessing must have a strong formative role. However, this does not prevent the use of summative assessing for certain specific purposes. For formative assessing to have the maximum benefit for learners (and teachers), again it must be carefully planned and undertaken. A mark or short comment on an assignment is unlikely to have much of a formative effect, whereas using an assignment (be it written, discursive or practical) to open discussion about learning, needs, or future learning, has a vast potential.

Process – product

Process and product in learning are closely related: there is unlikely to be any product without process; the product is likely to depend strongly on the process engaged in its production. Most assessment in education involves the judgement of some product, be it a loaf baked by learner bakers, an essay assignment, some technological structure or a PhD thesis. Products are easier to assess than processes. A tangible object is easier to judge than the ways in which a group of learners working together interact, come to know each other, become aware of individual strengths, weaknesses and needs, or how an individual explores how to become a self-motivating autonomous learner. Not only is the judgement of products a normal activity within our society, but in the context of education it also allows teachers to check and compare their results, the argument being that subjectivity is decreased. In areas of learning where process is considered important, formal assessing is less commonplace: for example, in aesthetic or literary appreciation, drama, discussion skills, learning to cope with new or unusual interpersonal situations, psychomotor skills, to name a few. As in most aspects of assessing, the aims of learning are important: if the aim is to learn to drive a car, then assessing which involves the learner writing an essay about the theory of driving is likely to be inappropriate.

We consider process assessing to be a very important aspect of learning. It is discussed further on page 97.

Criterion-referenced – norm-referenced

Using the example of assessing for mastery discussed earlier, we would more likely be happy if we knew that the pharmacist (or surgeon, or plumber or bus driver, etc) had reached a particular level of competence in his or her areas of skill, rather than had obtained slightly in excess of the mean mark in his or her final assessment before leaving college/training. It would be reassuring to know that the plumber had indeed reached a level of skill such that he or she was competent at, say, joining two copper pipes using a copper fitting and necessary tools.

In these, and many more examples of assessing learning, a score which merely describes the standing of the learner in comparison to his or her peers is of less use than a score which indicates the level of competence in a number of areas: of less use to the learner and probably of less use to the teacher and possible employer. The former approach is known as norm-referenced and the latter as criterion-referenced assessing. Stated simply:

— *Norm-referenced assessing* aims to compare the achievements of the learner with those of other learners.
— *Criterion-referenced assessing* aims to assess the learner by comparison with some predetermined or negotiated criteria.

Much has been written about norm- and criterion-referencing (see the bibliography at the end of this section). Many of the more esoteric articles attempt to define specific delineation of two distinct ways of assessing, arguing not only that construction, marking and analysis should be different for norm- and criterion-referencing, but also that each has its own associated mathematics. Here, we wish only to raise the issue that selection of these particular modes is an important consideration. It is more the way in which assessing is judged, than the actual instrument used, which indicates criterion- or norm-referencing. As always, the starting point should be to clarify what the overall purposes of assessing are: if an important purpose is to improve the learning of individual learners then we believe that criterion-referencing is the most appropriate mode. It allows both learners and teachers to judge a particular assessment against certain criteria. These criteria may be based on the products or processes of learning and could be unilaterally set by teachers, negotiated between learner and teacher, or devised by the learner him or herself: self-referencing, as applied in self-, and possibly peer assessing (see page 105). Whichever method is used, criteria need to be developed (as they do in norm-referenced interpretation) and results need to be judged.

Individual-focused –group-focused
Assessing focused on the individual aims to describe the individual, help him or her in his or her learning, and help the teacher arrive at a better understanding of his or her needs. In comparison, group-focused assessing aims to provide information about group trends and about overall 'standards', perhaps with

the hope of presenting generalized views of large groups so that individual idiosyncrasies and differences are blurred.

The majority of 'public' examinations (college entrance, those at 16 + and 18 +) are group-focused as are the various attempts to assess overall standards, such as the efforts of the Assessment of Performance Unit in the UK. Even much internal assessing undertaken within schools, colleges and higher education is group-focused: scripts are skim-read before deciding on the standard for grading; a pre-ordained mark scheme is used based upon group expectations. There is nothing wrong with this approach if it suits the purposes and aims of assessing, but as a method of facilitating learning it falls short. If we wished to assess whether or not a driver who left a public house at closing time is fit to drive, we would observe and assess the individual. It would be little use applying the group statistic that, say, 10 per cent of people leaving public houses at closing time are unfit to drive, therefore every tenth person should be arrested! If assessing is to help learners learn, it must focus on individuals, and must take account of individual needs, strengths and weaknesses.

Continuous –end-point
Continuous assessing is generally taken to mean assessing periodically throughout a particular learning process, a procedure which is becoming more commonplace in most areas of institutionalized education. By 'end-point' we mean assessing at the end of a particular learning process, for example a final examination, end-of-term test or assignment at the end of a course.

When discussing a formal mode of assessment, continuous or periodic assessing is meaningful: during a particular course, learners are assessed at intervals. Assessing may be through course work, examination, oral, written assignment, etc. Compared with end-point, this type of continuous assessing has certain advantages for learning. For most learners, it has the possibility of providing valuable formative feedback about their strengths, weaknesses and needs; it can help reduce stress associated with the contrived 'examination environment'; it can motivate them to do consistent work, and does not unduly penalize for one or two below-par pieces of assessed work. However, for such advantages to be realized in practice, the organization of continuous assessing needs to be focused on the needs of the learners. It is insufficient merely to set several essays rather than one, only providing a raw grade or mark as feedback. Likewise, several in-course examinations where only an overall mark is provided is likely to do no more for learning than an end-point examination. But with useful formative feedback, with discussion and analysis, the quality and process of learning can be improved; as always the approach and process of assessing is all important. Where much emphasis is placed on marks, grades, comparison and certification, some of the potential benefits to learning will be lost. Where only some assignments are identified as 'counting towards an overall grade' others are likely to receive less attention from learners.

When discussing informal internal modes of assessing, 'continuous assessing' can take on a new meaning:

— not only assessing at intervals, but also taking active account of the continual and natural processes of informal assessing
— using results to open discussion, share ideas and aid learning.

Assessing then need not be something 'done to' learners, but 'done with' learners.

Learner-judged – teacher-judged

In everyday life we are constantly judging events that directly involve ourselves or our peers. While the learner car driver is judged by his or her teacher, and later by an examiner (teacher-assessed), he or she also makes his or her own critical judgements of his or her actions and abilities (self-assessed). When the test is finally passed, friends will be all too willing to pass judgement on the new driver's abilities (peer-assessed)!

In institutionalized education and training, the majority of learner assessment is unilaterally undertaken by the 'teacher' who may be the person directly involved in 'teaching' the learners, or who may be external to the process (for example, an examiner in a public examination). Rarely are learners given the responsibility and freedom to assess and judge their own learning. Responsibility could be vested in individual learners, in groups of learners working together or in a collaborative process involving both learners and teachers. Self-, peer and collaborative assessing have important roles to play in the shifting of emphasis from teaching to learning. We consider these modes of assessing later in this section.

Internal – external

Internal assessing involves those actually participating in the learning/teaching process having control over the assessment.

95

Learners, teachers who are involved with the learners, and others closely involved in the learning process (perhaps parents, youth leaders, laboratory technicians) are all sources of internal assessing. External assessing on the other hand involves an 'outsider', someone brought in for the purpose of assessing. Such outsiders include examiners in public examinations, driving test examiners, educational psychologists, etc.

Where emphasis is upon informal, formative process, individual-focused or learner-judged modes of assessing, it is most probable that 'insiders' will be involved. Other modes may well involve internal or external assessing. For example, a formal, largely summative assessment may be undertaken by the learner's teacher, by an external teacher, or by a combination. The latter is common in higher education where an external examiner is appointed to moderate internally set and marked assessments. These assessments may be end-point (as in a degree examination) or may be continually set assignments. The role and power of the external examiner is variable, generally acting as adviser and arbiter rather than final judge.

While internal assessing is accepted in higher education and adult training and education, at other levels misgivings are often expressed. These are particularly strong in the case of end-point or summative assessing, where the main purposes are to classify and certificate. Here the argument that external assessing allows comparison with other learners and therefore provides the ability to monitor overall standards, both local and national, is often used. Moves towards this mode of assessing can easily be seen in many countries. For example, in the UK the Assesssment of Performance Unit has been set up by the government to assess and monitor standards reached by school learners. In some states in the USA progression of learners between grades depends on adequate performance; in most states units have been set up to monitor basic skills in the schools. Earlier liberal and learner-centred assessment systems in Denmark are giving way to systems which emphasize external standards in formal assessment.

Emphasis on external assessing does little to promote the type of learning we suggest throughout this book. However, internal assessing has an important role to play in helping learners learn, in helping teachers know the needs of learners, and in helping others (eg, employers) come to know what it is a particular individual can do.

We believe that certain modes are particularly appropriate to 'assessing for learning', in particular those which tend towards:

— criterion-referenced
— formative
— process
— individually focused
— internal.

Aspects relating to these modes are now discussed in greater depth.

Assessing process

In most areas of life, processes as well as products are all important. Likewise in much institutionalized education and training, process is a very important aspect, particularly when learning involves interacting, or when the learner is engaging in the role of generator or receiver described in Section 4. Assessing these processes can facilitate learning. Also, as we noted in Section 1, different learners have different preferred ways of learning; their processes of learning are different. Assessing these processes can help the teacher and other learners come to know each other, to understand better each other's needs and to minimize any mismatch between teaching and learning.

> Starting from a product (a loaf of bread baked by learner bakers) the learners and teachers involved discuss and assess the processes that went to make each loaf. For example, shape, size and finish are related to what was actually done during each part of making and baking. Learners are actively involved in constructive criticism and see it as a natural part of their learning process. Assessing in this way helps learners learn from each other's work and helps the teacher become sensitive to needs and problems.

Much informal assessing is of processes. The teacher writing a reference or report on a learner is likely to have formed opinions by watching process: how the learner interacts with others, the learner's attitude towards learning, the contributions made to group work, etc. The driving instructor watches what the learner driver does, modifying his or her instruction in the light of these processes. The learners in informally assessing their teacher are likely to focus on process: how the teacher teaches, rather than on product: what is learned.

However, most formal assessing of learners undertaken within institutionalized education is of products: the written assignment, a drawing or sculpture, the laboratory notebook. Even in those parts of learning where much emphasis is placed on what we describe elsewhere as 'loving' aspects (interpersonal development

97

of group dynamics, learning to help one another learn, working together), if assesssment is undertaken it is often of a written, reflective nature. This is not surprising as teachers are used to product assessment; it is easier to manage, more tangible and convenient, and easier to moderate than assessing process. Assessing process is more overtly subjective than that of the majority of products: it occurs in real time, and there is little or no chance of 'going back to check' or of 'taking it home' to assess. In much of real life (as opposed to institutionalized education) process is inferred from product: car crashes are reconstructed from their products, skid marks, positioning of vehicles, damage caused. Scientists often infer process from the effects, the products, of some change or interaction.

Many investigations into 'how teachers teach' concentrate on process. From observations of student teachers, to detailed and complex observation and interaction analysis, the focus is on process rather than product. For example, the observation schedule outlined on page 56 concentrates on various teacher/learner interactions. The outcome here may well be products: written descriptions of process, or video or audio recordings of the teaching-learning process which go some way towards providing a record for discussion and analysis after the event.

Within a more usual learner/teacher situation there are approaches to assessing, both formal and informal, which can facilitate development of process.

A major assignment for a degree course module in audiovisual communications involves the learners in a group television production. Learners work in groups of six to eight to develop a short recording of a topic of their own choice. The product is seen as less important than the processes involved. At the start of the assignment the teacher stresses that a major aim is to develop group interaction and co-operation, indicating that team work is necessary for a satisfactory production. Reasons for this approach are indicated and discussed.

During production, much emphasis is placed on discussion and negotiation, both between the group members and between learners and teacher. Those learners in other groups are engaged upon other work, but often act as consultants and observers to the group involved in production. Much work is undertaken outside timetabled sessions and learners are asked to keep individual diaries of what they do, how much time is spent, what problems arise and how these are overcome. At timetabled sessions, diaries are discussed between the learners and teachers, focus being upon what was done, how it was done and how this relates to the activities of other group members.

During practical TV work, many of the learners not directly involved, together with the teacher and technicians, observe, help and suggest alternative approaches. Emphasis is on facilitating group processes and encouraging learning, rather than upon an expert 'showing how it should be done'.

At the end of each session a discussion is held where learners are encouraged to reflect critically on the processes engaged in. Assessing is based on the observation of process, diaries of events and group discussions together with the product. It is negotiated between learners, technicians and teacher.

Assessing used in this way is of an essentially formative nature with focus upon involvement of the learners in the assessment process. It is obviously internal, involves both learner and teacher judgement and is a continuous process. The key to the assessing is communication between learners, between learners and teachers and others involved. In the above case study an overall summative grade (demanded by the course validation) is also given, based to a large extent upon the processes previously assessed and discussed.

The techniques of assessing process noted in the case study draw heavily upon those more usually associated with evaluating (see Section 2). Indeed, other techniques such as observation schedules, snowballing and brainstorming, lend themselves to formative process assessing, as do role play and simulation (for example an in-tray exercise where learners are presented with information about a particular issue or subject and asked to work either together or alone to reach conclusions or a decision). These techniques lay stress on the formative nature of assessing, which is now considered in more detail.

Formative assessing

As we have previously indicated, a formative mode of assessing aims to use the process of assessing to facilitate learning. This, we believe, must be a major aim of assessing for learning. Whether assessing is primarily criterion- or norm-referenced, informal or formal, process or product, to have a formative role there must be meaningful communication between assessed and assessor. To be really formative we believe that assessing must involve discussion between those involved: groups of learners or learners and teachers. Such discussion may arise during a number of activities: informal questioning during learning/teaching, groups of learners working together on a project or syndicate work, specific feedback from the teacher (or peers) about an assessed piece of work. If discussion can involve setting up the assessment aims and criteria, so much the better.

To help provide formative feedback to learners about their written assignments, the proforma shown in Figure 3.2 is completed by the assessor. This may be either the teacher or one or more peers depending upon the particular assignment.

These written comments are used as the basis of subsequent discussion between those involved. Generally, this discussion is undertaken individually between assessed and assessor(s). In the case of peers being the assessors, they may or may not invite the teacher to be present (in practice, they usually do!). If any issues of a general nature arise from these discussions, time is set aside for discussion with the complete group.

Although it may appear that this approach takes too much time, in practice this is not the case. Much learning is by learners working on assignments on their own or in groups rather than in more formal classes taken by the teacher.

ASSIGNMENT ATTACHMENT

Student's name:

Assignment Title: Unit No.

NOTES

Sections left blank are not relevant to this assignment.

Some aspects are more important than others, so there is no formula connecting the number of ticks in different boxes with the grade.

A tick in the left-hand box means that the statement on the left is true: a tick in the second box from the left means that the statement on the left is true to some extent. Similarly for the right-hand boxes. eg.

Topic covered in depth ☐ ☐ ☑ ☐ Superficial treatment of topic
means that the topic was treated somewhat superficially in the assignment.

Ticks in the right-hand boxes show areas of deficiency in the report.

Itemized Rating Scale

STRUCTURE   ←   →

All goals covered   Little relationship to goals
Topic covered in depth   Superficial treatment of topic

ARGUMENT

Accurate presentation of   Much evidence inaccurate or
evidence   questionable
Logically developed argument   Essay rambles and lacks continuity
Original and creative thought   Little evidence of originality
Relevant use of own experience   Little evidence of own experience

SOURCES

Adequate acknowledgement of   Inadequate acknowledgement of
sources   sources
Correct citation of references   Incorrect referencing

Figure 3.2

STYLE

Fluent piece of writing
Succinct writing

Clumsily written
Unnecessarily repetitive

PRESENTATION

Legible & well set out work
Reasonable length

Untidy and difficult to read
Over/under length

MECHANICS

Effective use of figures & tables

Figures & tables add little to
argument

EXPLANATION AND COMMENTS:

GRADE:

TUTOR: .... DATE: ....

Figure 3.2 *(continued)*

The above case study indicates one possible method of providing feedback to learners. There are many others. For example, comprehensive 'notes in the margin' or at the end of an assignment, verbal (or non-verbal) feedback during discussion in class, and computer-marked multiple-choice items, all provide feedback to the learner. Self-assessment questions embedded in learning material, or at the end of a section, can usefully cause the learner to reflect and self-assess.

It may not always be possible to achieve the contact and two-way communication we believe to be so valuable. In distance learning written comments from tutor to learner may be all that is generally possible. At times these could be supported by telephone or audioconference (see the Appendix) but this may not always be convenient. It is not the method but the quality and intent of feedback which is all important in helping learners learn. Feedback can have a very negative effect on learners as all teachers (and learners) know too well!

Collaborative, peer and self-assessing

Traditionally, most formal institutionalized educational assessing is controlled unilaterally by teachers who set the criteria, mark the learner's products and provide varying degrees of feedback to the learner and/or others. At the opposite end of the spectrum is the learner who undertakes a practical project or written work, sets his/her own goals, continually monitors his/her work against personally set criteria, and judges the final outcome. These two 'models' represent extremes of a continuum indicating the degree of autonomy vested in the learner for his or her learning, as indicated in Figure 3.3.

In education, little account is generally taken of the right-hand side of this continuum although it is continually incorporated in learning; for example the person designing and building a con-

Teacher controlled   Learner controlled

|———|

Most	Collaborative	Peer	Self
traditional	assessing	assessing	assessing
educational			
assessing			

Increasing emphasis and responsibility placed on the learner for their own learning.

Figure 3.3

struction in wood, developing their performance for a dramatic production, or writing an assignment. Here we focus upon this side of the continuum.

Collaborative assessing involves discussion and negotiation between learner and teacher about assessment criteria, methods and any grading. Peer assessing either involves discussion and negotiation between the learner and his or her peers, or may be assessment undertaken by one or more peers apart from the individual learner being assessed. By self-assessing we mean a self-directed and self-determining learner setting his or her own assessment criteria, judging his or her learning processes (or products) against these criteria, and making decisions based on these judgements. The learner also may well have set his or her own goals for learning, determined his or her own programme of study and performed the learning deemed necessary. This is obviously very different from the majority of educational and training assessing currently in use.

We see collaborative assessing as being the most immediately applicable move towards greater involvement of learners in the processes of assessing and facilitating learning. It is probably also more acceptable than self- or peer assessing to the majority of learners and teachers used to the unilateral autonomy of teachers. In collaborative assessing, the teacher and learner (and possibly also peers) are actively involved in the assessment process. There are a variety of ways this can be achieved in practice, from negotiating and agreeing all aspects of learning leading to a particular assessment, to negotiating final marks on a more traditionally teacher-set assessment.

> A major aspect of the assessment of an in-service diploma course for teachers and trainers involves 'integrative assignments', where each learner is expected to draw on concepts developed in a number of modules and relate these to his or her own work experience to produce an assignment for assessment.
>
> Learners are drawn from a wide range of backgrounds, and display a wide range of needs and expectations. To help meet these needs, assignment titles, content and assessment are negotiated between course tutors and learners. The process is a multi-stage one involving progressive focusing which culminates in a written learning and assessing contract between learner and tutor. The process varies over the period of the course; as time progresses greater learning and assessing autonomy is vested in the individual learners (here we focus on the aspects of assessing; further details of this study are given on page 145).
>
> Each module has one or more assignments associated with it, which may be written or may use audiovisual media. Completion dates and guideline starting dates for a term's assignments are negotiated with the

complete group. These take into account completion of relevant modules and aim to minimize 'bunching' of workload.

Prior to the starting date of a particular assignment, learners are asked to consider what it is they wish to do and to prepare personal notes outlining their aims, likely content and format of assignments. These notes include the assessment criteria the learners would like to use for assessment of their work.

Close to the agreed starting date, time is set aside for each member of the group to outline briefly their proposed assignment (including assessment criteria) to peers and tutor. The process is formative and highly supportive to individuals, who generally modify their outlines in the light of these discussions.

Individual learners and the tutor meet to negotiate a 'contract' which specifies details of the assignment and assessment. Details of assessment generally include:

— who will assess (peers and/or collaboration between learner and tutor)
— criteria for assessing (eg, against assignment objectives, impression, process, product)
— distribution of assessment grades.

Although agreed at this juncture, learners are free to renegotiate during the process of their assignment.

The assignment is handed in (generally on time: agreement and negotiation of dates places a responsibility on the learner not usually apparent in more unilaterally set work) and is assessed. Where collaborative assessing is the chosen mode, learner and teacher meet to discuss the assignment and together negotiate around the previously agreed criteria. Where peer assessing has been chosen, negotiation is either among the chosen peers, or between peers and learner.

It must be noted that the process outlined above is developed over a period of time, particularly where peer assessing is involved. Learners need much help and encouragement initially, but generally react very favourably as they become more familiar with the technique. The process has a very marked positive effect on the relationships between learners and teachers.

In the above case study, both the topic of the assignment and the assessment criteria are subject to negotiation. It is equally possible, although we believe less effective, to use collaborative (or even peer) assessing for judging assessments which have been set by the teacher. This may form a useful intermediate stage for many teachers, and could be applied to, for example, essay questions, problem-solving exercises and many forms of practical work. In the case study it is product which is being assessed; similar techniques could well be used for process. It is equally applicable to course work or end-point assessing, and is individually focused and formative.

We see peer and self-assessing in education as being very closely related, particularly where one is learning alongside other learners: self-assessing takes place in relation to the activities of peers, their goals, criteria, judgements, processes and products. Judgements made during self-assessing are modified by feedback from peers. This is likely to be so to a lesser or greater extent in most distance learning. Very little organized learning takes place in complete isolation from peers.

> Part of a training course for teachers involves personal presentations where each group member gives a 10- to 15-minute presentation of his or her own choice to a small group of his or her peers. Presentations are video recorded by one of the group. A major aim is to encourage group discussion about teaching styles. At the end of each presentation, the group replays recordings and discusses the presentation. Enabling and constraining factors are analysed and evaluated.
>
> In practice, groups are very supportive while at the same time generating much constructive criticism of use to both the presenter and other group members. Generally, learners indicate that they find the experience both useful and enjoyable. The group dynamics are certainly improved.

The use of self- and peer assessing in a formal context poses perhaps a large challenge to teachers and learners more used to a unilateral control and decision-making process in educational assessing. Nevertheless, we believe that both peer and self-assessing are important in the context of learners taking greater responsibility for their learning.

It will be clear from the preceding pages that we have purposely expressed a particular view about the modes of assessing most likely to promote the learner's responsibility for learning. Often these are at variance with the dominant modes found within most institutionalized education and training. We make no apology for this. In a move from teaching to learning, from learners receiving to becoming actively involved, from teachers performing to becoming conductors and facilitators of learning, there is a need for a large change in emphasis of assessing. The change must be supported by training, discussion and critical analysis among all those involved: teachers, learners, employers and parents. Finally, it must be remembered that assessing learners, whatever mode or method is used, can and should be used to provide valuable feedback to *both* the learner and the teacher about their needs and about their own successes and failures.

Criteria for assessing

The processes of judging an assessment are carried out against certain criteria. This is so whether the judging is the sole province of the teacher, a collaborative venture between teacher and learner, or undertaken by peers or the learners themselves. These criteria can be arrived at in a number of ways, via objectives, contracts between learner and teacher, or impressions.

The vast majority of learning and teaching is undertaken with particular objectives in mind, although perhaps not the formally written pre-specified objectives often discussed in educational texts. Criteria for assessing should be related to the objectives of learning. To take an extreme example, if the objective of a particular part of learning was to be able to recall four sources of assessment criteria, then assessing the learner's knowledge of the brainstorming technique would be a most inappropriate way of either facilitating or assessing the particular learning. This is obviously exaggerated, but how often is assessing not related to the objectives of learning? How often is a particular level of learning, for example problem solving and transfer of knowledge, assessed by methods which require straightforward recall of knowledge? Not only is the assessment an inappropriate way of monitoring the learning, but worse it is likely to have a detrimental effect on the learner's motivation to learn.

Where objectives for particular learning are specified and are known by both learners and teacher, these form a useful basis for generating assessment criteria. The idea is appropriate to all the modes of assessing we have previously identified. It is equally applicable to affective, cognitive, psychomotor and interpersonal learning, whether the learning experience is wholly negotiated between learner and teacher, an individual is working as an autonomous self-directing learner, or learning is controlled by the teacher.

The source of objectives against which to assess is ultimately the views, feelings and beliefs of those involved: the teachers, 'outside' teachers (for example examination boards, external examiners, moderators) and, it is to be hoped, the learners. These beliefs are a complex product of the education or training system, and the society within which the individuals operate.

Criteria arrived at through negotiation and discussion between learners and teachers can result in an assessment 'contract'. Criteria derived in this way are fully known and should be acceptable to both parties. The learner is involved in the assessment procedures from the outset, and therefore the criteria which are to be used for judgement should have a good relationship with the learning which takes place. Any apparent mismatch could well form the basis of renegotiation of the 'contract'. The case study on page 103 describes one particular application of contract-type assessing.

Impression (or romantic) assessing involves the assessor reading, looking at or discussing the aspect being assessed and deriving his or her comment or grade depending upon the impressions made. To a varying extent, most assessing has a degree of this approach, however objective one considers assessments are. Problems exist where the teacher is assessing unilaterally: the learner has little or no knowledge of criteria being used and therefore may be unable to respond in a meaningful way. Criteria and interpretation may well change from one assessment to another, again causing difficulties for the learners.

However, impression assessing can form a very good basis from which learner and teacher can discuss the assessment. Ideas and feelings of both learner and teacher can be explored, and the reasons for impressions and interpretations can be discussed.

Suggested group activities

1. *Why does assessing take such a key position in much education and training?*
Use a snowball or brainstorm technique (see Section 2). If possible try to include learners in the group discussing the question.

2. *Who is a particular assessment intended for?*
We have found that analysis of a case study is a valuable starting point. For example, one or more members of the group could be asked to bring to a meeting brief case study examples of who uses the results of a particular assessment. The whole group may discuss and analyse the case study, or alternatively sub-groups could report back after analysis.

3. *What modes of assessment should be used?*
A structured discussion could be organized using pages 88–97 of this section as a resource.

4. *How do you (or your department/institution):*
   — *add together marks from various assessments?*
   — *analyse the marks given in one or more assessments?*
   — *feed back results of assessment to learners?*
If you are working in a group all the better, particularly if the group includes some learners. Possible ways of facilitating group work for these activities are to use either snowballing or brainstorming (see Section 2).

5. *How can learners' attitudes towards a particular approach to learning be assessed?*

The group could be asked either to read an example case study (eg, that given on page 103) of a learning situation, or, better, focus on an example taken from one of the group members. Use either brainstorming or snowballing (see Section 2) to generate ideas which can then be discussed and evaluated.

6. *Design assessment procedures for a particular group of learners which will involve the learners discussing between themselves their own learning problems.*

The group considering this could be divided into smaller groups of, say, four to six people. Each could be asked to consider the same issue using a different technique. For example, one group may be given a case study example to discuss and transfer to their own area. Another could brainstorm or snowball; another could use the services of an 'expert' input. All groups should report back at the end.

Difficulties and criticisms

Assessing is currently viewed as being primarily for giving information to other educational establishments, employers or teachers on a succeeding course. The bases of these assessments are an explicit or implicit normal distribution (eg, 20 per cent of learners at 16 pass this examination, implying that is is passed by the top 20 per cent of the ability range and that a grade A or grade 1 will probably be about the top 4 to 5 per cent). While the examination may not have been designed with that in mind, it will probably be marked or moderated that way.

Even when teachers mark work which is handed back to learners and not used as part of the certification process outlined above, there is a tendency to give marks or grades on this basis. The comments made on a piece of work may be brief, encouraging or discouraging, but the learner has little idea of the basis of the mark, which is why we used an example of a feedback form to give the learner some reasons for the grade or mark.

The way that we have suggested using assessments is alien to current practice — the implementation may take more time and energy than current practice. The initial gains would be obvious. The change in relationship between learner and teacher would be considerable. The teacher's role would change from an expert pontificating to a mentor assisting. The change is also from a subject expert to a problem solver and facilitator of learning. Most training courses for teachers do not focus on problem solving; the courses are run using conventional didactic methods often associated with the 'sitting with Nellie' approach. Is a 50 per cent load on teaching practice the right way to train a teacher or should the training include a smaller load and much more time on problem-solving strategies? Obviously we are open to criticism for using a book as a means of trying to get learners into a problem-solving mode, although we hope that our recent students would recognize our own attempts to move away from a didactic approach.

We may have implied that current practices are wrong, whereas our own intention was to identify alternative practice which is focused on helping the learner to learn rather than comparing and reporting to others. We have also tried to show that alternative approaches enable more useful reporting. However, that change also implies that employers and others who use the results of assessing have to learn a new means of communication. With the plethora of recent assessment methods (graded tests, criterion-referenced tests, competency tests, profiles, personal records) employers are already raising their arms in horror and asking for a return to the previous diplomas and certificates which they 'understood'. The chances of moving a stage further is obviously loaded with difficulties. Are education and training about providing reports to outsiders or enabling the learners to learn? Are these necessarily incompatible?

A further inertia that the teachers experience is with competitive comparative assessing. Teachers are usually the ones who succeeded in the previous system so there is a certain pride in a system in which they succeeded. Is it a minority who are dissatisfied and are raising questions in the way that we have done? Why are national, state, county and local authorities moving away from the current comparative system? Has the system become so discredited with the general public that it is politically worthwhile to change? How does one persuade teachers who are often alienated by government decisions to see the pragmatic and political merit of change? Would there be improved communication with learners, parents and employers? How can the changed system be explained to those audiences? The explanation involves yet more work, the changed assessment system involves yet more work; where is the time coming from in a falling rolls and reduced finance environment? Won't the effort be at the expense of helping learners?

The assumption behind much of the assessment proposals is that the learners are willing and able to take on responsibility for their own learning and assessing. The evidence from current practice would suggest that the assumption is untenable, especially when associated with a steady increase in unemployment leading to further alienation from those in deprived urban areas. We can only provide the limited evidence available from mastery learning, tutor-based learning, resource-based learning, supported self-study, distance study, open learning and some management training. It is agreed that the motivation is high, but does the motivation lead or follow the methods? All these methods depend heavily on feeding back information to learners, assisting them in learning and giving them responsibility for their own learning and assessing.

Annotated bibliography

Ashworth, A E (1982)
Testing for Continuous Assessment
London: Evans.

Although the title indicates emphasis on continuous assessment, the text has wider applicability, examining briefly the reasons for testing, test design and construction, marking and statistical analysis.

Bejar, I I (1984)
Educational Diagnostic Assessment
Journal of Educational Measurement, 21, 2, 175-89.

The paper outlines the potential of microcomputers for enabling adaptive testing to improve the accuracy of self-referenced assessment. Two principal focuses of diagnostic assessment are noted: deficit measurement and error analysis. Deficit measurement focuses on areas where achievement is less than expected and has potential by using predictive strategies for present and future errors. Error analysis is seen as more clinical and less adapted to self-referencing. Error measurement is a problem for both styles of diagnostic assessment.

Black, H D and Dockerell, W B (1980)
Diagnostic Assessment in Secondary Schools
Edinburgh: Scottish Council for Research in Education.

This short book identifies what is meant by diagnostic assessment. The uses of diagnostic assessment are examined. Techniques for the construction of diagnostic tests are demonstrated, including the problems involved. The implications for teachers and pupils actually using diagnostic assessment are considered.

Boud, D (ed) (1981)
Developing Student Autonomy in Learning
London: Kogan Page.

Practising teachers working in higher education around the world describe their personal experiences of introducing alternatives to the traditional mode of teaching, course design and assessing. The issues of student, peer and teacher assessment are discussed. Case studies are given about the ways professional teachers have confronted the issues in areas such as independent study, self-directed learning and contract learning.

Boud, D and Lublin, J (1983)
Self Assessment in Professional Education
New South Wales, Australia: Tertiary Education Research Centre, University of New South Wales.

Outlines examples of self- and peer assessment and feedback in electrical engineering, law, architectural design and orthodontics. On the bases of the case studies and the attitudes of staff and students, the constraints and validity are considered. Suggestions are made for setting up such a procedure. There is an annotated bibliography of 126 items.

Brewer, I M (1985)
Learning More and Teaching Less: a Decade of Innovation in Self-Instruction and Small Group Learning
Guildford: SRHE and NFER-Nelson.

Describes an attempt by the author over a long period to examine and improve ways of promoting learning in higher education. The move from traditional teaching to a mixture of small-group work, problem-solving discussion and peer group interaction is described in detail. Assessment involves a wide range of techniques aimed at assessing learners' higher order skills in addition to the more normal recall.

Broadfoot, P (1979)
Assessment, Schools and Society
London: Methuen.

Examines the need for, and roles of, assessment within the context of schools (and other institutions) as a part of society.

Assessment and examinations are studied as instruments of social control and their effects upon everyday classroom life is explored. The origins of formal assessment together with newer developments in accountability, performance assessment and informal techniques are dealt with.

Broadfoot, P M (1979)
Communication in the Classroom: a Study of the Role of Assessment in Motivation
Educational Review, 31, 1, 3-10.

The paper examines the motivation of pupils, particularly the less able. The alienative effect of the assessment process is investigated. Assessment is used as a one-sided process rather than an interactive process. A view is put forward that continuous exchange of perceptions and evaluations should enhance motivation by (a) improving the status and self-esteem of the pupil; (b) encouraging positive thinking by the pupils about their progress; and (c) understanding the teachers' aims better. Some findings are given from a preliminary study involving pupils in their own assessments.

Burgess, T and Adams, E (eds) (1980)
Outcomes of Education
London: Macmillan.

Describes various systems of profile recording in schools and higher education. Outlines many of the problems and possibilities of profile recording. Contains many references.

Clough, E E, Davis, P and Sumner, R (1984)
Assessing Pupils: A Study of Policy and Practice
Windsor: NFER-Nelson.

The book examines overall school policies and formal procedures as well as day-to-day classroom practice. It reveals a confusing variety of approaches, unnecessarily complicating the teacher's role and bewildering pupils and parents. Suggestions are made to avoid pitfalls and co-ordinate assessment activities.

Ericson, D P (1984)
Of Minima and Maxima: the Social Significance of Minimal Competency Testing and the Search for Educational Excellence
American Journal of Education, 92, 3, 245-61.

The paper provides a critical review of the use of mastery-type tests based on criteria within the high school diploma. It identifies the problem that when large proportions achieve mastery the diploma is devalued. Who decides the arbitrary cut-off of mastery and non-mastery, and how can it be justified? The idea of such assessments being diagnostic and remedial conflicts with the use of the diploma to select those who are to progress to the next system or grade level.

Good, H (1978)
Interview Marking of Examination Scripts
Assessment and Evaluation in Higher Education, 3, 2, 122–38.

The paper describes a system of marking examination scripts in discussion with students. The argument is based on teacher accountability for the time spent in assessing students and a survey of staff and students who were involved in the process. It also enables feedback to students on end-point certification type of assessment.

Harris, N D C (1975)
What is Assessment?
Assessment in Higher Education, 1, 1, 5–12.

A brief outline of a variety of ways of viewing assessment: predictive, diagnostic, comparative, absolute, formative and summative.

Lublin, J R (1980)
Student Self-Assessment: a Case Study
Assessment in Higher Education, 5, 3, 264–72.

The paper argues for the importance of assisting students to be realistic judges of their own performance. Details of a case study are reported which investigated the self-appraisal abilities of a group of engineering students and showed the majority to be reasonably competent. The implications are discussed: less assessment for marks and more for diagnostic feedback are advocated.

Miller, C and Parlett, M (1974)
Up to the Mark: a Study of the Examination Game
Guildford: SRHE.

A study of examinations, their use, and students' reactions to a variety of methods used at Edinburgh University. The authors identify two groups of students: cue-seeker and cue-deaf students. In an environment where teachers are also examiners, the former group appear to be at an advantage.

Open University (1981)
Measuring Learning Outcomes (E364 Block 4 Education Studies)
Milton Keynes: Open University Press.

The book identifies the different purposes of measuring learning outcomes and the extent to which these purposes dictate the methods employed. The strengths and weaknesses of methods are considered and these are related to uses in the classroom. Ideas are given for designing tests, examinations and observation schedules.

Rowntree, D (1977)
Assessing Students: How Shall We Know Them?
London: Harper and Row.

A comprehensive and original analysis of the reasons for, and methods and effects of, assessing learners. Rowntree is constructively critical of much current assessment used in education and suggests that the purposes be re-examined with greater focus on learning.

Rowntree, D (1981)
Statistics Without Tears
London: Harper and Row.

A clear straightforward introduction to the range, scope and utility of statistics in education. The book does not concentrate on how to calculate, rather on the underlying concepts and interpretation of statistics.

Section 4 Roles of Learners and Teachers

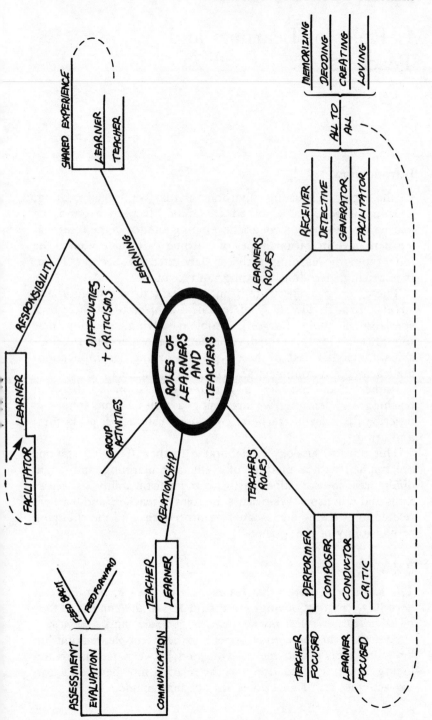

4. Roles of Learners and Teachers

Introduction

In the types of learning environment that we are advocating, learning is seen as a shared experience focused around the learner. In this section we are developing an idea of the roles that learners have in various types of learning. We shall refer to the four types of learning activity elaborated in Section 1 (ie, memorizing, decoding, creating, and loving).

These cover a spectrum from the taxi driver memorizing streets, through the study of technical subjects with their own specialist language (jargon), problem solving, creating new solutions and ideas, to the development of interpersonal relationships. Obviously each of these types of learning has implications for learning environments and the role of teachers.

Rather than consider a one-to-one relationship between teaching and learning we are using a series of metaphors to describe the roles of teachers: composer; conductor; performer; and critic.

This musical analogy is elaborated further. The expectations are implied with a mixture of systematic planning, individual differences, co-ordination, aesthetic and artistic ability, as well as skills and criticisms. We discuss the roles of teachers and learners related to assessing and evaluating procedures and the changing responsibility of the learner.

Roles of learners

The learning activities that learners carry out (ie, memorizing, decoding, creating, loving) are considered in the context of four possible learner roles: *receiver; detective; generator;* and *facilitator.*

At first sight there may appear to be a simple relationship between receiver and memorizing and between facilitator and loving. It is our contention that the relationships between learning activities and leaner roles are not that simple.

Receiver role

Let us consider the learner sitting in a lecture theatre or classroom being showered with words, pictures, diagrams, lectures, books, experiments, computer programs, face-to-face conversations, and television. There is an over-abundance of signals and stimuli to receive. The human brain filters out many of these signals. The learner has to create decoding strategies based on his or her own experience in order to cope with the filtering and rearranging of this wide range of data, information and experience. This filtering and rearranging enables the learner to make sense of the vast array of information, and to place it in his or her own context based on previous experiences from both within and outside institutionalized learning.

The receiver role may involve all of the learning activities. For example, from experience of previous learning, some learners may use a variety of note-taking strategies from headings and subheadings to mind maps, from mnemonics to picture association. Each is using strategies in a creative way to decode material to be memorized into a format which the learner feels can help him or her to remember. Unfortunately, learners often assume that a learning environment aimed at decoding is in fact aimed at memorizing. Learners may then use their energies and apparent role to focus on the wrong types of activity.

As we have noted above, the learner as receiver has a large amount of decoding to carry out. Here, decoding enables stimuli from print, experience or oral contacts to fit into existing life experiences and enables the learner to recode information back into an acceptable form, often via memorizing. The use of mnemonic and other memorizing strategies is a form of decoding. This decoding may involve creating new associations and interactions to aid memorizing.

The loving activity of learning is not out of place with the receiver role. Many learners find that involvement in syndicates with other learners can enhance their learning. In all aspects of memorizing, from cognitive to psychomotor, from affective to interpersonal, the assistance, support and criticism of a peer is often necessary.

Detective role

The detective is a different role where the learner again has a whole array of stimuli. However, the assumption behind the use of these stimuli is different: that of discovery. This discovery may not be new to experts, but may be new to the learner. Here, memorizing is used to identify strategies that were successful on previous occasions in searching, analysing and communicating. The decoding activity is obviously crucial in this role. Analysis may create 'new' information or result in the creation of alternative types of communication. Loving is also an important aspect in eliciting responses and assisting peers and others.

Generator role

The generator is the role where new ideas, new communications (particularly artistic), and new ways of viewing events are created. Again memorizing and decoding are important aspects. The memorizing is more subliminal, involving passive recourse to memory rather than actively recalling. Strategies, environments, and experiences which enhance the role may be memorized and recalled actively, but conventional cognitive and psycho-motor skills are probably not used so actively in this role. Decoding is crucial but more likely in the sense of decoding one's own thoughts, ideas and presentations. Creating is obviously related to the generator role, although that creating may be a long hard labour for some and a more spontaneous activity for others. The loving aspect is more doubtful in this role. Some people as generators need solitude and isolation (eg, some artists and writers) while others find social contact more essential.

Facilitator role

The facilitator role focuses on interpersonal relationships and helping others to learn. 'Others' may be fellow learners, colleagues or even teachers. Again, each of the four learning activities is involved. Memorizing is more about remembering names, individual sensitivities, likes and dislikes. Decoding is about watching for and feeling for tensions, visual and facial signals, listening for oral signals, feeling body space and territory. Creating involves using these decoded signals and providing personal signals which enable, inhibit, encourage or discourage interpersonal learning; creating harmony or discord. Many learners are lacking in personal skills such as initiating and terminating conversations. Are these skills memorizing, decoding or creating? It is clear that the loving activities of learning are the focus of the facilitator role.

From the above outline of the roles of learners, it is clear that there is also a multi-faceted role for teachers. Using the musical metaphor from the introduction, we now consider the roles of the teacher and in particular his or her future roles as we progress towards an information age.

Roles of teachers

Let us consider the musical analogy to describe four possible roles of teachers: *performer; conductor; composer;* and *critic.*

If we consider an orchestra, a band or a group of musicians, each is a performer: they work together (often with a conductor) to interpret the work of a composer. They are critical of the composer's work and of their own performance. They may also be critical of the performance of other similar groups; they may wish to identify a new creation to solve the problem that they have identified, or just to give pleasure or raise questions with fellow humans.

Teacher as performer

In much current formal education and training, the teacher as expert is in the performing role. Information is usually provided to learners by word of mouth. When we already have print how is it that we are so bad at using it that we have to reiterate it? Why do we present it to a mixed ability/background audience in an identical way so that few, if any, will find the pace or level anywhere near their need? The whole process is partly one of indoctrination into the ways of thinking in the particular discipline; the learner needs to learn the code to enable communication to occur with the performer through the written word of assignments or examinations. The onus may be put on the learner's shoulders, particularly in decoding activities, but the learner may well resort to memorizing for survival with little real decoding or understanding: the receiver role is being viewed solely as memorizing. Current assessment systems implicitly encourage the majority of learners to use this strategy because they can gain sufficient marks or grades for certification. As we move towards easier and easier access to data and information, the other three roles of teachers have more relevance.

Teacher as composer

The composer role is developing the range of learning experiences. Certainly not all of these can be preplanned and prephased. The needs of the learners are paramount.

The composer will design learning resources from worksheets to a range of books, magazines and other printed resources, from drill and practice computer-based learning to simulations and learning games based on the computer, from experiences with equipment and the environment to experiences with other people.

The design will include the assessment procedures, assignments, record keeping and will define the responsibilities of the learners in self-, peer and teacher assessment. The teacher will incorporate routines and experiences to enable the individual learners and groups of learners to develop their strategies of learning how to learn. It is not the haphazard design carried out by individual teachers (the members of the band or orchestra) but an overall mutual agreement on the composition that does not preclude improvisation and impromptu modes. The performers have become the learners with the teacher in their specialist role, rather like the leaders of the groups of instruments. (This relationship is considered further in Section 5.)

Teacher as conductor

The conductor role is a crucial role for the teacher of the future. It will be about enabling the group to learn how to learn in all areas of learning, how to organize, assess and evaluate their learning. The teacher as conductor will need to be a multi-disciplinary all-rounder with access to specialists when and where necessary. The specialist would act more as an adviser, consultant or leader in a particular context rather than a performer: the guest conductor brought in for a particular problem-solving exercise.

The musical conductor is about ensuring that the pace and balance are right. Different instruments and groups of instruments play at different rates and at different levels according to the characteristics of the instrument. The conductor role is about ensuring that each learner maintains self-assessment to identify continuously his or her learning roles and strategies suitable to his or her own characteristics. The teacher will facilitate the group of learners in following the learning design according to the constraints, abilities and environment in which learning is taking place. As we identify in Section 5, learners in classrooms and learners at home have different needs which may require as different a design as those for classical western music and classical Indian music. Diagnostic assessment procedures, together with evaluation procedures, will also need to be utilized by the conductor, but these are really the role of the critic.

Teacher as critic

The critic role is one which is shared between teachers, specialists and learners, rather than being confined to the teachers or conventional examiners. Self- and peer assessment will become more important parts of the assessment procedure. Assessments will be focused around reports presented orally, by electronic media and/or in print. These are the procedures outlined in Sections 2 and 3.

Relationship between learners and teachers

It is our view that much or most communication between teachers and learners should take place through the medium of assessment and evaluation. The assessment and evaluation can be formal procedures or informal procedures such as conversations (see Section 2). The assessment and evaluation procedures may have a fixed routine, but they should not be so fixed that variations are not possible. It is necessary to adapt and adopt ideas and strategies which are relevant to that group of learners in that context; no two groups are alike even in the same context, nor is the same group identical when in different locations or with different teachers. The dynamics of the group changes with relative body positions and certainly changes when different members are present; change the teacher and the group is different! Group dynamics also change when the room layout or physical environment are changed.

Evaluating and assessing can be used for the purposes of both feedback and feedforward. One of the hopes of the early programmed learning advocates was the idea that a programme could be adaptive to individual learners. By keeping records of the learner's achievements and errors it was considered possible to begin to predict which of a variety of routes would be more suitable for the learning that was about to be undertaken. This prediction is the feedforward aspect. But the feedforward needs to be associated with a continuous feedback as well to enable continuous adaptations to be made.

The programmed learning approach and much of current computer-assisted learning are still based around the memorizing and decoding activities of learning. In order to move towards an adaptive approach, an enormous amount of storage is required within a computer. There may be more potential in adapting more complex artificial intelligence approaches. There is available an excellent adaptive processor which can make instantaneous decisions and has the ability to communicate well with humans: another human! However much computer-based learning is adapted, using current or future known technologies, there is no way that it can match the human in adaptability and in dealing with human problems.

Why should the teacher be the sole keeper of records? Why shouldn't the learner take more responsibility for record keeping? Why is it that this is most common in junior and elementary schools and least common in universities? If the learner is keeping a personal record, who is being cheated when the next phase of learning occurs and incorrect information is there? Obviously this raises many questions of styles of assessment, personal records, profiles, competency-based approaches, criterion-referenced approaches, as alternatives to conventional norm-referenced assessments for comparative purposes. Are we still in a society which requires a standard industrialized system for an information age?

It should be clear that we see the learner being involved in taking on more responsibility for his or her learning. The creating and loving activities of learning are more important in a world where less hours are likely to be worked each week, for less weeks in the year, for less years in one's life. The role of education as a continuing lifelong process involved in adapting and coping with change is different. The role of the teacher as a performer will become more redundant. The teacher as composer, conductor and critic relating to the learner creating and loving, but with memorizing and decoding as adaptable, looks to be a more likely scenario in the future.

Suggested group activities

1. *What roles do we expect our learners to take?*
A video recording of a teacher with learners is the basis for this activity. The teachers explain and discuss what they see in the video. The four learning activities of memorizing, decoding, creating, and loving may be used as a basis for discussion. The same sort of session could be carried out with learners; their perspectives are probably even more illuminating!

It is important that this is seen as a creative and loving session, not as a critical and destructive one. Nobody is perfect and we all have something to learn from one another. The process is about helping one another to develop and adapt.

2. *What roles do we take; do they vary?*
A similar video recording could be used to that outlined in the

previous activity. The focus of this activity is what roles teachers take. The four roles of performer, composer, conductor, and critic may be used as a basis. The activity could again include learners as participants if possible.

Again, it is important that this is seen as a creative and loving session, not as a critical and destructive one. The process is about helping one another to develop and adapt.

3. *How do continuous assessment procedures relate to the roles of learners and teachers?*

Ask one of the group to identify both formal and informal assessment procedures that they use with a group of learners. As individuals, consider each of the assessment procedures from the perspective of the roles of the learners (receiver, detective, generator and facilitator) and the roles of the teacher (performer, conductor, composer and critic). Compare perceptions.

An alternative is to use a case study as a basis.

4. *What sort of feedback is given to learners, parents and employers?*

Using learners' marked work, reports sent to parents, or reports/references sent to employers, critically review what use these are from the perspective of the recipient.

Role play could be used where the 'learner' (having only seen comments on their own work), the 'parents' (having only received the report) or the 'employer' (having only received the report or reference) are in conversation or formal interview.

5. *How do we enable groups of learners and individuals to develop autonomy in learning?*

Where teachers are practising this approach, both they and some of the learners could give a brief presentation and then be available for questioning.

6. *How much jargon do we expect learners to know?*

It is essential that the members of the group are from a mixed disciplinary background. Resource material can be handouts used in, or a video recording of, an actual lesson. Non-specialists should look for technical jargon and unreasonable assumptions. The issues identified could form the basis for a discussion with the originator, or, if material used is drawn from outside the group, for members to side within judgement based on cases made for the prosecution and defence.

Difficulties and criticisms

The stance we have taken has focused on the learner. Most education and training involves teachers too! Not only do the characteristics of the learner have to be taken into account but also the characteristics and personality of the teacher. Unfortunately, current organization and administration of education and training often fails to avoid the weaknesses, or build on the strengths, of the individual teacher's personality. The ideas that we have proposed may enable some teachers to function more efficiently than at present, but teachers who are good in the performing role may feel very frustrated by changing to the conductor and critic roles.

The section has taken a particular stance with regard to giving more responsibility to learners in learning how to learn. For learners already involved in an institutional system where this is not the case, a change will either have to be dramatic (with all the inherent problems of such a change) or gradual. For a learner changing the learning environment the dramatic approach may be most fruitful, but considerable support will be necessary in the initial phases.

As learners are often unaware of their own best style of learning or their optimum work cycle, effort will be necessary over a period of time to help them to find out more about themselves. The focus of that exploration is limited by times and styles of working. Rather than imposing alternatives from the teacher it is better if learners can find out from one another by sharing how they work when studying, reading, problem solving, etc. Again this approach is more time consuming. We contend that the improved performance of learners in the long run more than compensates for the loss of performance in the early stages.

Learners have been trained to work alone; any sharing constitutes cheating. That is a clear barrier that will need to be broken down if the approaches suggested are to be implemented. The losses include less assessment information about the individual; the gains include learning to share problems and explorations with others, not being dishonest about learning, viewing learning as a shared activity. Should the assessment tail wag the learning dog?

The musical analogy for teachers' roles can, like all analogies, be carried too far. If the score is poor in classical music the sound is not pleasant. If there is too much volume from brass and drums at the expense of others, we complain of noise. Noise is a useful concept in learning and in communication: if there is too much noise the message is lost. Noise in a learning context can include:

— unpleasant environment (humidity, temperature, sound noise)
— assumptions beyond the learner's abilities
— incompatibility of learner and teacher values
— distraction (eg, learner has a headache).

Unless the noise is controlled, the communication process breaks down. Also, what is acceptable to one learner may be noise to another.

We have suggested assessing and evaluating as means of ensuring that communication exists. They may not be regular formal procedures, but as indicated in Section 2 they can be informal procedures. Returning to the musical analogy, the critic can be reacting instantaneously rather than writing a script for a television programme a week later.

Annotated bibliography

Barrett, J (1984)
Student-Tutor Communication in Radio Tutorials
Programmed Learning & Educational Technology, 21, 4, 333–5.

This paper considers the way that students can hear one another interacting with the tutor, using a combination of FM radio and telephone. Tutor and student talk during these tutorials is outlined and analysed based on various courses: Learning Skills, Australian Studies and First Years of Life. The students participated most in Australian Studies where they were more familiar with the content. The paper should be considered along with that by Guiton in the same issue of the journal which describes the more technical aspects.

Bawden, R and Valentine, I (1984)
Learning to be a Capable Systems Agriculturalist
Programmed Learning & Educational Technology, 21, 4, 273–87.

The course described focuses not only on systems agriculturalists but also on those agriculturalists being autonomous learners and effective communicators aimed at helping others and building up good interpersonal relationships. The course uses two learning strategies in two contexts. The contexts are staff initiative (gradually decreasing) and student initiative (gradually increasing); the latter involves the use of co-operative groups. The assessment is based around a student and employer-initiated competency profile including peer and self-evaluation of learning.

Brewer, I M (1985)
Learning More and Teaching Less: a Decade of Innovation in Self-Instruction and Small Group Learning
Guildford: SRHE and NFER-Nelson.

Describes an attempt by the author over a long period to examine and improve ways of promoting learning in higher education. The move from traditional teaching to a mixture of small group work, problem-solving discussion and peer group interaction is described in detail. Assessment involves a wide range of techniques aimed at assesssing learners' higher order skills in addition to the more normal recall.

Buzan, T (1982)
Use Your Head
London: BBC Publications.

The book explains discoveries about the human brain and helps the reader to understand more clearly how his/her mind works. It includes tests and exercises to improve reading power, memory, studying effectively, solving problems more readily and ways of thinking. The well known mind maps (otherwise known as coral diagrams, patterned notes, etc) are a feature of the book.

Clough, E E, Davis, P and Sumner, R (1984)
Assessing Pupils: A Study of Policy and Practice
Windsor: NFER-Nelson.

The book looks at overall school policies and formal procedures as well as day-to-day classroom practice. It reveals a confusing variety of approaches, unnecessarily complicating the teacher's role and bewildering pupils and parents. Suggestions are made to avoid pitfalls and co-ordinate assessment activities.

Entwistle, N (1981)
Styles of Learning and Teaching: an Integrated Outline of Educational Psychology
London: Wiley.

Provides an overview of those aspects of psychology related to an understanding of how learners learn. The book is a good starting place for someone new to this area of psychology or who requires a summary of research findings. Many references are provided.

Gibbs, G (1981)
Teaching Students how to Learn: a Student Centred Approach
Milton Keynes: Open University Press.

The focus is on students learning from one another. By learning from peers with the same problems on the same course, the gap between them is less than that between most students and tutors. Examples are provided for carrying out the process, often using a snowballing approach.

Harris, N D C (1979)
Preparing Educational Materials
London: Croom Helm.

The book emphasizes the careful development of educational materials and learning situations to aid and develop student learning. The lecturer is perceived as taking on four roles: composer, performer, conductor and critic (designing learning materials, lecturing, organizing learning situations and evaluating his or her own design and management). Some theoretical background is provided along with case studies of practice.

Hill, W F (1978)
Learning Thru' Discussion
Palo Alto: Feareon.

A small book which gives a ten-stage system for organizing discussion particularly related to discussion around papers that are provided. The system involves focusing on problems of comprehension and the main messages of the paper, leaving the criticism until near the end. The final focus is on the group's performance.

Jaques, D (1984)
Learning in Groups
London: Croom Helm.

The book addresses the questions: How can tutors in post-secondary education improve their skills in leading group discussions? How can the tutor play a less dominant role? How can students be encouraged to treat seminars as a co-operative venture? Theory and practice are linked by case studies including alternatives to the traditional tutorial and seminar.

Merrill, M D (1984)
What is Learner Control?
In Bass, R K and Dills, C R (eds) *Instructional Development: The State of the Art II*
Dubuque, Iowa: Kendall/Hunt.

Many examples of learning assume that all students should receive identical instruction; this idea is either untenable or unsupported. The paper addresses the idea of enabling the students to decide on the various mediational tracks and which they will use. Several aspects of student-controlled instruction and display selection are received, and a model for display processing is developed.

Rogers, C R (1983)
Freedom to Learn for the 80's
Columbus: Charles E Merrill Publishing Company.

The book derives from an earlier book *Freedom to Learn*. The goals are to provide a climate of trust in the learning environment. Decision making is seen as participating and enabling students to build their confidence and self-esteem and to develop into lifelong learners. The teacher is seen as a facilitator. The book is aimed at fully functioning people, whether teachers or learners.

Rudduck, J (1978)
Learning Through Small Group Discussion
Guildford: Society for Research into Higher Education.

The book is divided into seven chapters. Each chapter is written in two parts: the issues and the evidence. The book covers the range from students' roles and training students in small-group work to the leaders' roles; also included are monitoring small-group work and leaderless groups. The book covers a range of aspects from basic practical matters to more philosophical and psychological issues.

Wilson, B E (1984)
Knowledge and its Acquisition: an Introduction and an Overview
In Bass, R K and Dills, C R (eds) *Instructional Development: the State of the Art II*
Dubuque, Iowa: Kendall/Hunt.

The paper considers the acquisition of knowledge, based on the approaches of experimental, behavioural and cognitive psychology. In particular it focuses on the ways in which individuals differ in their abilities and approaches to the acquisition of knowledge and the resulting implications for course design.

Section 5 Meeting the Needs of Learners

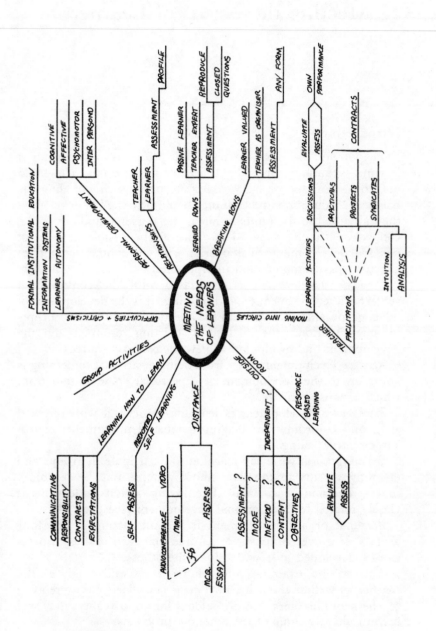

5. Meeting the Needs of Learners

Introduction

Education and training have particular problems in the design of learning situations. Should the learner be encouraged to build only on strengths, or on weaknesses, or how should these be balanced? Education and training should be aimed at developing the individual to the limits of his or her personal abilities in the context of the learning. There are four possible aspects of personal development which overlap with one another: cognitive; affective; psychomotor; and interpersonal.

Cognitive development is associated with the conventional subject matter in education and training. It is the development of the conceptual framework and the ability to apply those concepts in new situations, the analysis of existing resources and the development and evaluation of new ideas and resources.

Affective development varies from being aware that something is going on to the development of a personal value system from which actions originate.

Psychomotor development is learning associated with physical skills and co-ordination: playing a musical instrument, neuro-surgery, tree felling.

By *interpersonal* we mean learning to participate in groups and enabling groups to function; those groups may be learning, making decisions, socializing. The 'loving' activity in learning is closely related to interpersonal development (see page 21).

Personal or self-development is the interaction of the four aspects. It is over-simplistic to assume that each of these aspects can be developed independently of the others.

This section examines the relative roles and needs of the teacher as well as the learners. Let us consider some stereotype teachers and learners that are seldom found in reality; they will help to identify some of the potential problems.

The teacher of 40 years ago was probably nearer to a stereotyped army sergeant. A very authoritarian stance was assumed where the learners were expected to remain as silent receivers while wisdom was poured forth. The learners were probably expected to memorize everything off by heart in order to repeat it word for word without error.

Probably the other extreme of the spectrum is the supposedly trendy modern teacher who tries to become one of the group, although from a different generation with different values and experiences. The learners may not be at all clear what is expected from them and have to rely on their own resources and ideas without the guidance that they have come to expect from a teacher.

Considering the learners we can also look at two extremes. There are learners who expect the teacher always to know the answer and to rely entirely on the teacher for guidance, advice, criticism and encouragement. The learner expects every piece of work that has been written to be marked with a clear mark or grade and a set of statements that outline what has been done wrong and how the work can be improved on the next occasion.

Probably the other extreme is the learner who thinks that the teacher does not know anything, has lead a sheltered middle-class existence, and does not have any ideas about the problems and difficulties that learners experience while trying to come to grips with the particular learning. It is clear that there could be some poor matches between the learners and teachers that have been sketched above!

Today young people in transition from institutionalized education to adult and working life are effectively locked into the educational system beyond the compulsory sector in order to accumulate qualifications and/or work experience as a basis for being considered for paid employment. The serried rows of passive learners is an inappropriate technique in this context because most of these learners have rejected the conventional institutionalized education. It becomes important for the learners to have more control of the pace and style of what they do. The planning should be co-operative and reflective using peers and teachers. The use of project methods or of intrinsic motivation can enable better learning. The teacher becomes a guide understanding the competencies young people need for the outside world. The teacher becomes a person who will accept learners' participation in decisions rather than an authoritarian imposer of knowledge.

A working document of the European Community Action Programme on the transition of young people from education to adult and working life suggests three headings as a focus for learning:

1. *Individual and personal*
   — self-knowledge: strengths and weaknesses, mental and physical
   — self-confidence and autonomy
   — ability to use and accept criticism
   — initiative
   — logical capacity: decision making, problem solving
   — living with emotions
   — understanding and development of physical and health capabilities
   — development of manual skills.
2. *Interpersonal*
   — understanding of and feeling for others
   — ability to discipline oneself to accept the rules of a group or organization
   — ability to articulate ideas in words and to communicate, to listen, to explain, to read and to write.
3. *Understanding and knowledge*
   — understanding of number and basic mathematics
   — understanding and knowledge of existing kinds of work and of the organization of industry, commerce, and administration; possible developments in the future such as information technologies; and implications for the kinds of personal and interpersonal competencies needed
   — understanding and knowledge of the alternative forms and patterns of human activity that might replace 'work' and of leisure activities
   — understanding and knowledge of the nature of personal and family relationships
   — understanding of and knowledge of society as a whole and the individual's role in it.

The assessment implications in the context of learning can immediately be evisaged by scanning the above lists. Conventional certification with global marks would be meaningless, although some parts of the list would lend themselves to the specification of criteria by which judgements could be made. The criteria could be the basis for a profile, but much of the recording must be in the form of a personal record. The implication is for a personal assessment showing one's own development against the pre-stated criteria.

An alternative approach to assessment, in this context, is to use other learners as the assessors (ie, peer assessment; see page 102). The criteria for assessment can either be imposed or negotiated. We contend that criteria which are negotiated provide a better basis for most learners. The negotiation could, for example, involve potential employers.

In this section we examine various types of learning situations, discuss their characteristics and relate these to styles of assessment and evaluation which will help the needs of learners to be met.

Serried rows

The teacher is facing the learners who are usually in serried rows of seats either in a classroom or in a lecture room or lecture theatre (see Figure 5.1). The teacher is assisted in his or her teaching by the use of chalkboards, overhead projectors, slides, film, television or other audiovisual aids. The whole arrangement implies that the teacher is the expert performer and that the learners are in a receiver mode. The usual method of presentation (a loaded word in itself) is by passing on information. The learner usually writes notes. The partial assumption is that there are facts, a specified body of knowledge or an exposition, which will

SERRIED ROWS

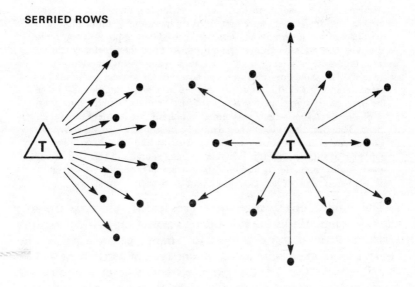

Figure 5.1

indicate to the learners the sort of work that they are expected to produce.

The learner's role is almost exclusively passive. The teacher is the purveyor of knowledge, the expert, the king of the subject. The approach is authoritarian, the teacher is the senior partner in the learning, and the learner has no real responsibility but to reproduce the expert's ideas. The assessment will most probably ask for the work to be reproduced and for examples to be worked out based on the presentations. An alternative will be where a range of reading is provided and the learner has to decide the purpose of the exposition and deduce what will be asked in the examination. This alternative does pass more responsibility to the learner in moving from a receiver to a detective role.

The learner is not expected to have much initiative, but to adopt the 'right answer syndrome'. Probably one of the key criticisms that can be levelled at this type of education and training is that the learners are expected to get the right answer; yet, as has been indicated in an earlier section, much of life is about finding the answers to problems that do not have a right answer or even a best answer but an answer that depends on the assumptions that the solver makes.

> In some textual material it is the practice to incorporate questions into the text. The questions can be used to check what has been learned (self-assessment questions) or to focus attention for learning. In a course on road safety, the learners were first given six questions to think about and then had to jot down any answers they considered applied. They could also talk to one another about the questions. They then had a synchronized tape-slide sequence and illustrated texts (using similar visual images). The same questions were the headings for the sections of the two presentations. After the sequence, the learners were individually asked the original six questions together with further more detailed questions.
>
> The first set of questions was aimed at helping the learners focus their ideas. They were questions which could be identified as 'to aid learning'. The learners' minds were partially focused by the questions. There is evidence to suggest that this is a very efficient method of learning, being more understandable to learners than a set of objectives. The more detailed questions were focusing on what had been learned.

The implications for assessment are clear. In this type of learning environment it is unreasonable to expect the learner to think for himself or to transfer ideas that have been learned in one context to another. The most suitable type of assessment will be the closed question (multiple-choice, short answer or structured essay-type question) where it is clear that a correct answer is expected. Marks are to be gained by using the expected method of solution, criticism or style of writing. Where the derivation of a solution involves an algorithmic approach, there will probably be only one or two potential algorithms assumed in the mark scheme. This style of assessment is most common in public examinations for certification because the assessments are the most reliable where discrimination is required between the learners. By implication it could be argued that the right way to teach for this style of assessment is to use the style of teaching that we have called 'serried rows'.

The assessment used is often incompatible with the teaching approach. Learners are often required to answer examination questions with open-ended essay questions, questions requiring analysis, and even generation of original ideas, whereas the teaching has developed an assumption of uncritical acceptance of ideas. In order to enable learners to cope with the style of assessment, different teaching methods are required, although the cynic might identify that the purpose of the assessment is to discriminate. If discrimination is required, let natural abilities flow rather than teaching for the examination . . . what happened to the learning and the needs of the learner?

BREAKING ROWS

Figure 5.2

Breaking rows

Many classrooms and lecture rooms are used by the teachers in a different way (see Figure 5.2). The learners are given an active role in the learning by using buzz groups of four with a particular question or short problem. The groups may work on a snowball principle (see page 47), but will usually be expected to report some or all of their decisions to the rest of the group. The first implication of this approach is that the learner's views are valued and that other learners have something to offer the group. The teacher becomes less of an expert but takes on a role of the organizer of the activity (conductor). The feedback that the learner offers in his or her reporting gives the teacher some information about the particular problems of individuals and also of the group in general. Not only is the learner using some assessment procedures but also some evaluation procedures. Evaluation procedures are given in more detail in Section 2.

The learning is no longer about memorizing, so there are implications for assessment: opinions and evidence to support those opinions have become important. The assessor is trying to elicit the understanding demonstrated by the opinions, evidence and peer criticisms. The multiple-choice type of question may appear to be redundant. However, by using multiple-choice questions with a narrow range of distractors, learners can be asked to select the best answers (not the right answers) and justify their choice. Not only can the choice and justification be used for tutorial support to individuals, but also as a basis for small groups of learners arguing out the choice and perhaps even reporting a consensus view to their peers and the teacher for criticism. Similarly, short answer questions with reasons have similar potential. The focus of the assessment has moved towards helping learning rather than certification.

Structured essay questions (where the last part aims at opinions and experiences), open essays, case studies, projects, gaming and simulation have much potential for helping learning. The last few provide a better match between the mode of learning and the mode of assessment. The form of assessment will be similar to the form of learning, giving more security to the learner. The learner knows that the answer depends on assumptions and arguments using evidence; that evidence may have been provided or it may have had to be found. The learning and assessment can obviously be carried out in groups, but more of that later.

Let us also consider some of the alternative methods of structuring work when breaking rows. Worksheets have become increasingly popular at all levels of education and training. These vary from highly structured, so that it is difficult to get a wrong answer (almost reminiscent of programmed learning texts), to very open with a large amount of initiative required from the learner. The learner knows enough about the game of education and training to use these materials to hoodwink the teacher into thinking that he understands the material by returning it in slightly modified form in the assessments that are used for the course. In the present climate where more and more assessments are set by teachers, the skilful learner uses these handouts in order to adjust his or her communication to that which is acceptable.

The technique of the teacher setting the examination has probably been more prevalent in higher education than in any other level of education or training until recent times. A reason for attending lectures is in order to find out what it is that the lecturer is likely to set in the examinations. Those who are good at working out the expectations are those who succeed in the examinations... perhaps a legitimate way of sorting out the sheep from the goats, but not what the learning process is really about. Many of those who are successful in the higher education examination system find out that their knowledge is actually very superficial when they become teachers and find that they never really understood much at all, but merely succeeded in taking the examiner and themselves for a ride!

Where a teacher has political bias, there can be problems associated with some internally set assessments for certification. Again the learner finds out what the teacher's views are and succeeds in writing these views in order to succeed. The very clever learner may well deliberately take the opposing view in order to try out his or her own skills and abilities at arguing, but this is the exception rather than the rule. The example just given is a rather more insidious than explicit form of authoritarian teaching. The learner is really being given no more freedom than in the obviously formal lectures in the sciences and technologies. It should be clear that the teacher's role is gradually shifting from the controller of all communication and the sole communicator, to the controller of some communication, to an equal member of the group. Once the learning moves outside the room, at a distance or learning on one's own, the teacher's role changes even further.

Moving into circles

The obvious form of teacher and learners interacting is group work where the teacher is present. The group is often given a task with which to work. The teacher may become a member of the group in trying to complete the task (see Figure 5.3). In higher education it is possible for the teacher almost to become an equal member of the group when compared with the learners. The group may well be able to look at its own performance in undertaking the task; the group is then assessing or evaluating its own performance. The assessment or evaluation will be aimed at improving the group's performance on a future occasion. It will be noticed that the group has changed its aims; it is concerned with the improvement of the group functioning as a group rather than just the completion of a task. The learners have taken on the role of facilitators.

When a group moves into this mode the role of the chairman, particularly if that is the teacher, becomes more difficult. There

MOVING INTO CIRCLES

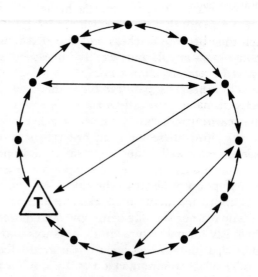

Note: only some cross circle communications are shown.

Figure 5.3

142

is no way that the teacher can completely abrogate his or her role or position, although some may be able to make that role less important. The group is trying to move towards equal members with the teacher as a member of the group. The evaluation and asessment that will now take place are more about the performance of value roles in the group. The group is learning about interacting with other learners and coping with their status, value positions and enabling each member of the group to play a part in the functioning of the group. It is sometimes valuable to get two parallel groups to work on a similar topic from quite different strategies. We have found it useful not to warn the groups that there will be any differences.

> The whole of a group of learners studying educational technology briefly discuss the role of educational technologists. The group splits into two, each with a leader. One group is given a paper about the role of educational technologists and is asked to use this as the basis of a structured discussion. The second group uses a brainstorming session in order to generate and later discuss the role. The two groups meet together in order to exchange ideas and are rather surprised by the other group's differing ideas. Not only are the groups encouraged to consider the effect of the way in which each has come to its decision, but also it enables the leaders to spend some time discussing the ways in which groups operate from a theoretical viewpoint.

The groups described above are continually evaluating their performance and the individuals are also evaluating their individual performances. Evaluating has become very much an integral part of the learning process. We advocate the use of this type of evaluating and assessing as an integral and important part of any educational or training process.

Another learning strategy in which the learners are in groups, but with less obvious teacher involvement, is during practical work where the learners are working in small groups. The learners are given a task and required to complete it in a fixed time (perhaps one or two hours). The task and reporting may be shared. The assessment is usually associated with the reporting aspect, although we have seen a particularly motivating assessment where learners are assessed by answering a series of questions at a computer keyboard. Feedback is instant, remedial help can be obtained when needed, and a record is automatically made for both learner and teacher.

In syndicate work the learners are given a task which they are asked to carry out in a fixed time. The group may again work on their own for this limited time but then report back. The reporting and the purpose of the exercise will probably be based mainly on a particular problem or critical review to be completed. It is less likely that the group will have any explicit help or guidance in the way that the group can begin to function. Most of us prescribe a mode of operation to save time (eg, snowball) but also to overcome any digressions about the way that the group functions. Unfortunately, the academic subject development often takes priority over learning and using interpersonal skills.

Probably the most extensively used learning strategy which starts with the teacher, followed by responsibility being put upon the learner, is the project method. It is difficult to decide whether this sort of learning is best described as resource-based learning or interaction. Projects are usually the development of ideas or the design of artefacts when the learner is given much more time than is usual in the educational system. The learner may be required to generate his or her own ideas or to choose from a range. For assessment purposes it is often thought more convenient to have learners working on their own rather than in a group. We consider this is unfortunate.

Projects can be assessed by one or a combination of four methods: *romantic, objectives, ranking,* and *collaboratively* (see page 105). It seems surprising that projects are given as individual learning tasks because most of us carry out our work in collaboration with others. There are already assessment procedures used to see how we perform as individuals; why use the project to assess individual work again? The potential for learning is enormous in projects undertaken by groups. There is seldom any advice or assistance given to learners in developing the group working together, yet surely part of the assessment and feedback given to the group should be exactly in this aspect. The focus often tends to be upon purposes and products rather than the all important processes. The collaborative method of assessment easily enables group goals to include process. As this involves a different type of learning and assessing, it is clear that the teachers and the learners will need to discuss and negotiate the whole process. One of the common traps that teachers fall into is to forget that the learning and assessment procedures are a new experience for each group of learners. If a checklist or contract arising out of collaborative assessing is to be used, it should be explicit and seen by the learner. Assessing within the learning process will be more informal and may be nearer to evaluating whereby the learners and the teacher are about improving the way in which the group develops. The teacher may be considered part of the group for all or some of its activities.

A major aspect of the assessment of an in-service diploma course for teachers and trainers involves 'integrative assignments', where each learner is expected to draw on concepts developed in a number of modules and relate these to his or her own work experience to produce an assignment for assessment.

Learners are drawn from a wide range of backgrounds, and display a wide range of needs and expectations. To help meet these needs, assignment titles, content and their assessment is negotiated between course tutors and learners. The process is a multi-stage one involving progressive focusing which culminates in a written learning contract between learner and tutor. Although the process varies over the period of the course, and may well be different for different individuals, there are certain common features:

1. Completion dates and guideline starting dates for a term's assignments are negotiated with the complete group. These take into account completion of relevant modules and aim to minimize 'bunching' of the workload.
2. Prior to the starting date of a particular assignment, learners are asked to start considering what it is they wish to do, and to prepare personal notes outlining their aims, likely content and format of assignments. Assignments may be written or may be based on audiovisual or computer media. More guidance and help are given for earlier assignments.
3. Close to the agreed starting date, time is set aside for each member of the group to outline briefly his or her proposed assignment to peers and tutor. The process is formative and highly supportive to individuals, who generally modify their outlines in the light of these discussions.
4. Individual learners and the tutor meet to negotiate a 'contract' specifying:
   — the assignment title
   — format(s) to be used
   — aims of the assignment
   — probable content
   — time-scale for completion
   — likely help needed (eg, tutorials, AV support)
   — an outline-marking scheme relating to the aims of the assignment.
5. Meetings take place between learner and tutor at intervals depending on individual needs. During these meetings, aspects of the initial contract may well be renegotiated.
6. The assignment is handed in (generally on time: agreement and negotiation of dates places a responsibility on the learner not usually apparent in more didactically set work) and is marked in consultation with the learner.

It must be noted that success of the technique outlined above depends upon the group's dynamics and relationships between learners and tutors. These are developed over a period of time. Anyone attempting negotiated learning or assessment must be aware of and sensitive to this.

Another group of learning strategies involve serious games, simulations and role play. Detailed discussion of these areas is beyond the scope of this book and those interested are recommended to consult one of the appropriate books listed at the end of this section. However, certain facets of learners coping with these strategies may be of interest. Much of education and training revolves around rational planning and analysis at the expense of intuition. The role of intuition is often not only underplayed but even excluded. In games, simulations and role playing, intuition plays a key role but not to the exclusion of analysis. Effective intuition should be rewarded (a form of assessment) leading to an analysis by the learner of the relationship. Similarly, ineffective intuition should be discarded by rational analysis.

The interrelationship between intuition and analysis is crucial with intuition often providing the potential for extending analysis from familiar limits. The procedure inevitably incorporates assessment within it. The evaluation is more likely to occur using peer observers and/or by a formal debriefing session where evaluating is again an inherent part of the learning process. Without analysis it may be difficult to separate assessing and evaluating from the learning process. Perhaps assessing and evaluating should be an integral part of all learning.

It is in the area of assessment for learning that the training of teachers and trainers is weakest. The learners on such courses are often told in lectures or in groups what is good practice but that practice is often omitted from the course itself. It is particularly in teacher training courses that we ought to be weaning learners away from dependence on the lecturers and tutors towards self-dependence both in their learning and in their creative powers of generating learning experiences for the learners under their ultimate guidance. The next generation of teachers and trainers will be in the world of information technology. Can they adapt to that world without being given the opportunity to find out, to learn for themselves and to pass on new ideas to their learners?

Moving outside the room

The teacher may be using resources in any medium from which the learner carries out some study on his or her own or with other learners, but where the teacher is not necessarily present. The teacher may be in the same room dealing with some of the learners, or the learners may be in a resource centre, a library or at home. This approach is often called resource-based learning.

The learners in a school are using a resource-based learning approach. Each learner takes a pre-test comprising multiple-choice and short answer items prior to entering the system. The test checks:

1. That they are able to cope with the prerequisites for the course.
2. That they are able to cope with the ultimate requirements.

Learners who fail aspects of (1) will be required to do remedial work (also resource-based) in order to master the prerequisites. It is seldom that a learner is successful on (2). When it has occurred, the teacher has provided more advanced work using books and journals. Each learner has a record card. On that card they mark their progress through the units.

Learners do not necessarily have to follow units in sequence neither do they have to do all units. The teacher has a master routing plan which identifies core units, remedial units and extension units. Some units may be carried out by individuals, some in pairs, some in groups of four, some may require a search in the library.

Each learner is allocated an initial unit (most will probably start on unit 1 unless the pre-test has shown that it is unnecessary). The teacher will draw up or give a contract of expectations together with a task card to the learner. When the learner has completed the unit he or she may check his or her own work against a master example or may request an assessment with the teacher. If the learner is successful then he or she will be allocated to another unit. The teacher may also write notes on the record card for his or her own and the learner's benefit. (In some systems the teacher has a separate set of record cards.) At the end of the set of units there may be a post-test in addition to the in-course tests. The whole technique is often based on a behavioural approach, but does throw much more responsibility on the learner for his or her own learning.

The learners obviously have much less assistance and help from a 'teacher' than would occur in a conventional teaching situation. Assessing and evaluating are essential in order to give the learners some feedback. Most forms of resource-based learning include diagnostic-type assessments that enable the learner to answer relatively straightforward questions so that there is some indication of progress. Many of the ideas originate from behavioural approaches such as programmed learning. This type of resource-based learning is recognizable by the use of simple yes/no type answers or multiple-choice questions. The learners will get a response from the book or the microcomputer which tells them whether their performances are satisfactory to enable them to progress.

There are also forms of resource-based learning where the learner goes to the teacher in order to complete an assessment. That assessment may be marked by the teacher or by a proctor (a learner who has already experienced the course, such as in the Keller Plan). Again the learner will be told whether his or her progress is satisfactory to enable him or her to progress to the next part of the learning. It will be noted that in all the examples quoted above the learners have little responsibility for their own assessment. There is also usually some form of record card or storage where the learner's progress is noted. In a modified strategy, the learner checks his or her own answer against a model answer and then has to make a decision whether to continue or not; some guidelines may be provided in order to help the learner to make the decision. Yet another strategy uses what is called an assessment matrix (or geomatrix). The learner may choose several answers from the matrix. After the learner has chosen, there is a discussion based on the choice of answers. This is not such a prescriptive right/wrong approach to the learner.

Self-instructional material we would see as something different where the learner may have very limited access to a teacher. There will be some similarity between this and distance study. The learner may make an appointment to use these types of learning materials at a centre. Because the material has to stand on its own, it is important that it is self-sufficient. The self-sufficiency could imply that it is important for the learner to have some sort of check before starting the learning to ensure that the prerequisite assumptions are met. Where possible it may enhance learning if there are two learners working together; there can be an added advantage that the materials need to be less detailed in structure and design because the learners help one another by discussion and joint attempts to resolve any problems.

The management of resource-based learning materials presents the teacher with rather different problems from those in a conventional classroom. It is necessary to keep a careful record of the progress of the learners and where they are in relation to the available resources. Most formalized schemes have some sort of decision tree, record cards or checklist. These management facilities may be operated exclusively by the teacher, by both teachers and learners or sometimes only by the learners. The method of management may depend on the role of the learner perceived in the scheme. It is possible for the learner to be perceived as a submissive receiver of information or as an active detective for his or her own learning.

The words 'independent learning' are sometimes applied to these schemes. In our opinion few if any schemes are genuinely independent in their entirety. One or more of the following is usually controlled by the teacher or by the designer:

— objectives
— content

— method
— mode
— assessment.

Perhaps it is helpful to remind ourselves of the teacher's roles:

— Composer, where the teacher designs the learning resources
— Conductor, where the teacher acts as manager of the learning
— Performer, where the teacher is the presenter
— Critic, where the teacher is checking the course for effectiveness.

For resource-based learning, using this analogy the teacher is primarily the designer or the composer. There will be a tendency to enable the learner to have a clear feedback on his or her progress. In turn this will tend to push the learning materials towards the prescriptive and also to push the learner into a passive and submissive role. It is necessary to encourage learners out of this mode if the ultimate aim is to enable them to learn how to learn.

The more carefully the materials are designed for a particular style of use, the more possibility that there will be a mismatch between certain types of learners and the materials. For example, material designed with the holist type of learner in mind (see page 14) may comprise several different sources of information about the same topic: perhaps photographs, video recordings, written information presenting alternative views, self-assessment questions which approach the 'problem' from various perspectives, etc. A learner who finds difficulty in moving away from serialist-type learning is likely to find this material difficult to comprehend and is likely to become frustrated, losing the motivation to learn.

Similar mismatches can arise when teachers attempt to use resources designed for a particular mode of use which is not their preferred style. Many teachers, for example, find it difficult to use resources produced by certain curriculum development projects which have taken a particular view of learning.

Distance learning

Those situations where the learner and the teacher are not in direct face-to-face contact, but are only in contact through a medium, we have called 'distance learning'. The learner will usually be at a distance but need not necessarily be so. The more obvious means of communication are mail, telephone, television and computer. Combinations of these are also possible. Some writers call this area 'remote interactive learning'.

Mail or correspondence learning has been used for many years. The main problem is the time delay in returning any work done by the learner. In order to make the response more meaningful to the learner the response needs to be more structured and detailed than would be the case with the learner who can have a face-to-face discussion after the work or the assignment has been returned. Two general techniques have been used, multiple-choice and essay.

The multiple-choice type question has the advantage that it can be returned on the day it is received if there are adequate facilities for marking and communicating. For example, it used to be marked by a clerk, but these days an optical reader is often used which scans the responses. Further points for discussion or additional work by the learner according to the responses to the multiple-choice questions can be included. With computer access through telephone, co-axial or optical fibre cable or satellite, access becomes potentially faster and more interactive.

The more common style of assessment uses essay-type questions or short answer type questions. These have to be handmarked by the tutor. Potentially there is much more opportunity to interact than with a computer-marked assignment in the multiple-choice format. A hybrid form is called a geomatrix question where the learner has to choose a set of statements from a matrix. According to the group of questions that is chosen, it is possible to generate a discussion-type response to the learner. The more sophisticated versions (eg, some used by the Open University) even incorporate responses from the learner, for example, whether he or she found the question easy, and whether he or she found the particular part of the course easy or difficult. The tutor now has some further information from the learner about his or her feelings as well as progress.

To take the best advantage of the system, the learner in this sort of learning situation needs a lot of help in learning. If possible, learners should be encouraged to contact one another by telephone, by audioconferencing, by meeting, or by having residential periods of study arranged.

A course for social workers combines periods of study in their nearest college, followed by periods of working in the field with a local social worker who had not attended the college course. At intervals there are short residential courses for all the workers. These workers are scattered over a mainly rural area of about 100 square miles with little public transport.

The telephone is used not only to keep line management informed about how the course and its participants are progressing, but also to enable regular contact between the tutors at the different colleges. The learners have a correspondence-based course for the times that they do not have college-based learning. This is a hybrid system with the potential for breakdowns in communication reduced at the planning stage and with a continuous assessment and evaluation procedure built into it.

The previous paragraphs introduced the idea of using the telephone for assessment and learning. There have been several examples of this type of work across the world. Much of the use has been in further, higher or adult education.

An interesting type of distance study is where some learners are on campus and others are learning similar (or the same) material but at a distance. In Australia, and other countries where small parts of the population are isolated by large distances from centres of population, such methods are used from primary through to university education. Children at home may receive only correspondence material or they may be linked by radio, television or telephone. Radio and television usually act as one-way systems, although there are some methods of using switching for two ways, or using unused side bands for piggy-backing responses.

An alternative feedback method uses a radio transmission system from the tutor in a studio. Students had a one-way telephone line to the tutor and were not directly connected to other students. Questions and problems could be telephoned in, heard by the tutor and by other students by means of the radio transmission. Obviously such a system is cheaper than multiple two-way radio or audioconferencing but requires specially designed equipment! Evidence suggests that students play a bigger part in telephone tutorials than in face-to-face tutorials.

Audioconferencing enables a group of learners to interact with one another and with the teacher. The way in which this is best organized is still not entirely clear although experience shows that, for a group in the early days of this style of contact, a prescribed agenda with some constraints on time concentrates the mind wonderfully! As a group becomes more familiar with the process so it can evolve its own procedures in much the same way that a face-to-face group does. Where there are mathematical or scientific tables or graphical displays, it has to be decided whether these are circulated prior to the meeting or whether video techniques are used at greater expense. The use of audioconferencing still presents several problems. For example, the relationship between the teacher and the learner is a crucial part of the learning process but is difficult to develop where the telephone is the only contact. (For further details of audioconferencing see the Appendix).

Video has two potential areas of use in this context. Using slow scan video, data can be transmitted by cheaper means than by using the normal bandwidth required for television. The documents are scanned and transmitted a 'page' at a time. The development of computer-computer communication allows two-way interaction between the teacher and the learners. This enables instantaneous reactions in much the same way that a note-pad or a chalkboard would be used in a one-to-one tutorial or in a small group tutorial. The use of such devices has enormous potential for discussion in relation to assignments both on an individual basis and where general problems have arisen, particularly as costs fall and accessibility increases.

Mediated self-learning

An obvious example of mediated self-learning is the use of a textbook by a learner working at home on his or her own without access to a tutor. The book will have been designed by the author in such a way that is rational to his or her view of the materials. However, it has to be borne in mind that the learner is often not the real consumer of a textbook as far as the sales are concerned; the purchaser or the person who recommends the book may be the tutor, teacher, trainer or lecturer. These people will view a book in a different light from the learner because they are probably already experts in the subject area. The learner may have some assistance where questions are used in the text. These questions may be in the text as revision for what has just been read or to focus attention on what is just about to be read. Probably the ultimate in trying to organize the book explicitly for the learner is a programmed learning text. However, with attention given to a step-by-step build-up of ideas the programmed text is suitable only for the serialist type of learner (see page 14).

Another approach is to give the learner an outline of what is to be learned together with how and why it is going to be approached. The learner then goes into the text with some pre-conceived ideas of what it is all about. Again the assumption is that the learner is receiving the wisdom from the writer. These advance organizers are imposed from outside the learner and not generated by the learner. Obviously there are places for both approaches; neither is the right or the wrong approach. A lot depends on the needs of the learner and the assumptions and requirements of the training or educational system in which the learner is placed.

From the last paragraph also comes the idea of following the objectives with questions which check that the learner has been 'successful' in his or her learning. The idea of feedback is common to most learning designed using a behaviourist approach. In its simplest form there are straightforward questions with a choice of two answers; a slightly more complex form uses multiple-choice questions. From the answer selected will be advice on what to do next. A more complex form is the matrix of statements described earlier.

An alternative form of feedback will be to generate a set of questions oneself before or after reading the text. This form of feedback obviously has the weakness that the learner may be having difficulties with the requirements in any case and will therefore be unable to formulate questions that help the learning process. The next step for this learner is to try and discuss his or her problems with a colleague, a member of the learner's family or preferably with another learner doing the same learning in the same context.

So far this section has assumed that the textbook is the only form of mediated self-learning. Many people learn from radio and television, from educational programmes, documentaries, drama and even the news! A form that is becoming more common is the home computer with its associated software. Again the software shows similar characteristics to text except that the learners are usually the sole consumers. The use of simulations where there is not a right answer is also common with the computer as it is in textual form. The feedback is dependent on the decisions that the learner makes. However, most simulations do have built into them certain assumptions about the learning process and the type of solution that is better; this may be considered to be more subtle rather than the explicit control of a behavioural approach.

A motor car manufacturing company wished to increase the knowledge of its sales, reception, stores and repair sections in all its distribution centres. There were two basic purposes: (a) to prevent ordering of incorrect parts with the associated cost, delay and frustration; and (b) to give customers more confidence in the service offered which would ultimately increase sales. It was too expensive regularly to fetch all the staff to the training centre, although the current courses were to be maintained. A form of learning was needed which could be used at the distribution centre but without a tutor.

The company decided to use interactive video together with printed materials. Each distributor was provided with the necessary equipment. Each new development in the cars (eg, a new progressive braking system) was the basis for a short interactive video programme with demonstrations of the effectiveness, details of the installation, replacement parts and servicing. The video had questions embedded, some of which required working with the text, others with the materials that had been shown on the video. It was possible to re-access previous parts of the video using a menu-type index. There was no formal assessment, but managers were required to keep a record of the use made by their staff and by themselves too. These records were regularly sent to headquarters.

One of the potentials of the computer is to use an approach that enables the identification of problems in the learner's attempts to learn a particular facet of a subject. The idea is that a variety of questions is given to the learner. As the learner makes errors then the computer makes attempts to identify possible causes of the errors and uses other questions to check out those errors. As can be seen, the idea is interesting because it does not assume one algorithmic form of solution or of learning. However, the practical problems of building up such a bank of diagnostic questions is horrendous. It also assumes that learning is about reception. The idea would probably fit into either mediated learning, resource-based learning or distance learning, depending on the roles of the learner and the teacher. The idea is one of many potential uses of the work done on artificial intelligence applied to learning.

Learning how to learn

It should be clear from the previous pages that we have a particular view about learning and the place of assessing and evaluating in that learning process. Our view is that the learner and the teacher should negotiate the learning tasks and resolve between them the best approach for that learner. The learner and the teacher will have certain expectations which may be very different. It is important that these expectations are resolved into a common agreement. That agreement should involve the assessment procedures: what is expected, why, by when, in what form so that there is a type of contract between the learner and the teacher, any variations in that contract should be negotiated. The assessment or the assignment will be a form of demonstration that the contract has been met. There is no assumption that the assignment is only about presenting a complete piece of work; it can involve the process of getting to any completed form or may only be about part of that process where the learner may complete it if required but that completion does not form part of the assessment. Whatever the assignment it is important that some form of response is given. The response may be in the form of marks, but could be a combination of a profile of achievement and an elaborated comment. In some cases the learner may be required to write a critique of his or her own work and even to assess it him or herself with the teacher merely giving a reaction to that critique. Another alternative is for the learners to assess each other's assignments. Obviously the use of peer assessment has problems but is probably a much more useful way of facilitating learning.

> A group of mature learners had followed part of a course where all the goals were prescribed. Their written assignments were judged against these goals. A later part of the course required them to identify their own goals. The learners worked in groups of three or four. Not only did they set their own goals, but also checked and criticized one another's. By working together in this way they were also able to identify common ground. Part of the assignments from each group were carried out as a joint responsibility. The assignments were self-assessed (some guidelines were offered, although not necessarily used by all) and then peer-assessed. These assessments were used by the tutor. The tutor was involved in the negotiations on goals particularly where groups felt that they were attempting too much. The assessments together with the assignments were read by the tutor. Had there been any disagreement, a renegotiation with the individual and the group would have been necessary. However, the individuals and the group were much more critical than the tutor.

One aspect of assessment that is often forgotten is the sharing of insights, problems and strategies between learners. Again there is the potential for a snowball technique where the learners share the ways in which they went about the assignment (see page 47). The development of this approach is towards learning being a co-operative venture between learners rather than something which is private and not to be shared. As a result of the co-operation between learners there comes a realization that each learner is different and that each learner's requirements are different: there are learners' personal needs which may vary from time to time; there are learning strategies to be identified... whether one is a serialist, a holist or able to vary between the two. Added to this is the need to value other learners' needs and their strategies without an assumption that one is right, the other wrong, or that one is inherently better than another.

One problem that can occur when the learners are given more responsibility for their learning is that the pace of learning can get slower and slower. Not only may fixed negotiated contracts be required of what is to be done, but also the time-scale in which it is to be done. When learners are required to exchange assignments so that they can learn from one another too, peer pressure is very effective for ensuring that deadlines are met, especially if a session is put aside for exchange within small groups. In an institutionalized, classroom-based, time-oriented educational system, these pacing pressures can override the individual's needs.

Another problem is that learners, particularly the more mature ones, set very high standards for themselves when given responsibility for their own learning and for exchange of assignments. There can be a tendency to fall into the trap of working without rest or relaxation both in the above context and to gain qualification for employment. Not only do learners need to find methods and strategies suitable for them, but also they need to know something of their own personal body rhythms and their own most efficient ways of working. Some learners need to work in short stretches with regular breaks, some work best at written work in the morning, some in the middle of the night! Some learners need relaxation at regular intervals, others need one or two days each week of complete rest. Some need background music, some need silence and isolation, some need other people around. Learners need encouragement to identify where, when (eg, time of day, time of week, time of month, time of year) and how they work best. Compromise will obviously be necessary.

Another important aspect of learning to learn is to find one's way around the information sources that are available. Taken in its simplest form the learner should be encouraged to look at textbooks or resources other than only those recommended: different learners learn best in different ways using different sources. The next step is to be aware of the range of resources that are available at the right level. Are these accessible or are only a limited number easily accessible? How can one access those that are less easily available? How does one use the sources when one has found them? The use of contents, index, skim reading, and checking diagrams, are all part of the learning process which can be fitted in with appropriate assignments so that the learner has the opportunity to find these things out. The next phase is note-taking both from texts and from the spoken word, whether the latter is highly structured or not. Again these are skills that the learner should develop with assistance from other learners and from the teacher.

A college agricultural course was designed to produce 'autonomous, holistic, problem solving' systems agriculturalists. The assumptions were that human beings seek whole person enrichment through active learning and make meaning of learning as an individual. Learning was perceived as being a process akin to problem solving and situation improving. The teacher tried to design a suitable learning environment where learners were facilitators of learning. The learning strategies and assessment were designed as a cycle of experiential learning. The learners were given a competency matrix in which they had to demonstrate evidence of being an autonomous learner, a systems agriculturalist, and an effective communicator (which incorporated helping others to learn). The learning strategies were student-initiated in co-operative groups. The assessments covered a wide range including a portfolio (self- and peer-assessed), quizzes, self-assessment questions, modified essay techniques (also used in medical education) and interviews. As a result the students produced a competency profile for use with future employers.

The final aspect of learning to learn is that of communicating, whether it is by the spoken or written word, by non-verbal communication or by other means such as electronic media or the various arts. Again these are becoming more common in courses especially after the age of 16... why not at an earlier age too?

Suggested group activities

1. *Can we design strategies for learning (say a maximum of one hour of learners' time)?*
Individuals, pairs or groups design learning particularly for: breaking rows, moving into circles, moving outside the room, learning at a distance, learning on your own. The learning should include appropriate assessment. The strategies developed are brought back to the main group for constructive peer review and modification. The strategies could then be tried with a surrogate or real group of learners, and reactions and assessments used as simple bases of evaluation. Further cyles of modification, peer and learner review can be carried out.

2. *How good are learning materials?*
Existing learning materials that are used or about to be used should be critically reviewed for:

— learning assumptions (eg, serialist, holist)
— memorization, problem solving
— learner as vessel to be filled or autonomous
— reading levels
— layout
— appropriateness of assessment
— adaptability
— resources needed
— prerequisites (both in the subject and allied subjects).

It is preferable for two or three to review the same material, compare notes and devise a consensus (if possible!) report which is made in writing or orally to others.

157

3. *How do you read?*

You should have a short paper available (say about reading). The paper should be fairly conventional in format with an introduction, elaboration, and a summary. A modified snowball technique is used. Readers are given, say, ten minutes to read the paper, but are interrupted after three minutes and asked to say what the paper is about. In pairs they discuss briefly what they have found (maximum five minutes). Reading continues with as much note-taking, annotation, underlining, etc, as the participants wish. In pairs they highlight the main issues. In fours they change tack and explain to one another how they read the paper, why they read it that way, why they took notes and how they took notes (eg, underlined, annotated). Finally they are asked to report between groups on how they could get the most information out of the paper in the shortest time.

4. *Which teacher role do you enjoy most?*

Using the analogy of conductor, composer, performer, critic, individuals are asked to choose two which they enjoy and jot down why. In pairs differences and explanations are explored. In fours any attempt at consensus may be difficult, so differences and disagreements could be the focuses for reporting.

5. *How do audioconferences work?*

With a fixed agenda, supporting papers and using telephones at home or work, try it! We suggest a maximum of 30 minutes. (See page 166 for further details.)

Difficulties and criticisms

Most institutionalized education takes place in buildings which are designed to enable certain types of teaching and learning to take place. As we have already identified, the serried rows of seats in a lecture room or lecture theatre provided visual signals of the roles to be played by the learners and the teacher: receiver and performer respectively. How realistic is it to attempt to overcome the inertia and difficulties raised by the environment? In addition, the administrative and organizational structure of most learning institutions is hierarchical and the learners can be viewed as the focus, but that focus may be lost in the flurry of administrative and academic decision making. The view of the learner as the customer or the partner in learning is less prevalent. We have argued that assessing and evaluating can be used as a means of changing the views, and roles, of learners and can help facilitate innovation in teaching strategies.

A larger barrier probably originates from the background and training of most teachers throughout the teaching situations we have considered. Most of the teachers have been selected because of their expertise as specialists in one way or another. The specialization may have evolved from their own studies for higher qualifications or from employment and work experience. Because of the specialization, the teacher not only has the role of expert but also speaks and writes using specialist language. There are two potential hurdles to communication and learning where the learner is given more responsibility for his or her own learning; the specialist has to curb his or her expertise and reduce his or her jargon. These are not easy changes, and will need a lot of co-operation between teachers and development of new relationships between teachers and learners. Again the development of assessment and evaluation strategies which depend on these changes could be one means of enabling innovation.

Much of formal education is beginning to feel the effects of falling rolls, and training is beginning to feel the effects of changing roles where the trainers may have had short or long spells of unemployment. The current institutionalized educational and training systems need to adapt to these changes as well as to a continuing need for retraining during working life. The current 5 to 15 year lead time from idea to implementation, as practised in the public sector of secondary and higher education, will need to learn from the much shorter lead times in the training and further education sectors, without falling into the trap of resorting to a didactic style of teaching.

Distance learning techniques are becoming more common than in the days when there were only correspondence colleges providing such courses. The design strategies used for distance learning courses and for resource-based learning may have to be adapted on a more widespread basis. The teacher, designer, assessor and tutor are less and less likely to be the same person. It is perhaps sad to reflect that there have been tendencies to revert to a cognitive subject-based curriculum in the secondary and higher education sectors at a time when the impacts of social and technological change point to the need for cross-disciplinary, rather than uni-disciplinary, approaches.

We have already used assessing and evaluating as a basis for suggestions to enable some of the changes necessary. However, virtually all teachers at all levels of education and training have been used to competitive forms of assessment. The move towards enabling learners to learn does not require assessments devised for comparison with other learners, but assessing against criteria. From these criteria are devised such assessment procedures as mastery tests, competency-based testing, graded tests and so on. Who decides on the criteria and how are they tested? If the decisions are made by the people who are already experts, there are obvious pitfalls. Two of these are: tests which are too simple, enabling all to pass; or standards set too high enabling too few to pass. In between those extremes are norm-referenced tests! In a learning context the resolution is feasible if assessing is viewed as a co-operative venture with learners rather than an exact science performed on learners.

Probably a more difficult problem is the communication of mastery, competency, profile and personal record types of assessments to people outside the education and training system. The use of profiles of assessment for trainees within an organization is already quite common. The use of these alternative systems of assessing as a basis of reporting to employers outside the system is a major hurdle. There is no longer a simple means of making an initial decision. The onus is thrown upon matching the profile to requirements, and the potential of matching someone with a AZBMNQ profile to a BWQHFR job requirement may be difficult!

The final questions are crucial to all that has been written in this book. Is the individual more important than society? Do education and training systems which focus on the development of an individual to fit into society lead to the scenes we have seen with the Nazis and the Khymer Rouge? Who controls whom and why? Assessment and evaluation are crucial tools in moulding the answers to those questions, but that is another story, the subject of many books and papers. The impact of information systems makes instantaneous access to records feasible. What are the needs of the individual learners? How can these needs be met?

Annotated bibliography

Abt, C C (1970)
Serious Games
New York: Viking Press.

The book explores the ways in which games can be used to instruct, inform and educate through the experimental and emotional freedom of active play united with abstract thought.

Ausubel, D P, Novak, J D and Hanesian, H (1978)
Educational Psychology: a Cognitive View
New York: Holt, Rinehart and Winston.

A detailed discussion of the ways in which individuals learn. The book provides much information of direct relevance to improving the quality of learning, from structuring learning materials and aids to analysing learning styles.

Bales, R (1970)
Personality and Interpersonal Behaviour
New York: Holt, Rinehart and Winston.

The book is based around a general approach to the understanding of personalities and groups in their natural settings. The main focus is on interaction process analysis but the book also includes less technical methods which are easily adapted to a variety of settings. Part I deals with analysing interpersonal behaviour. Part II identifies 27 types of group roles and their value directions.

Bawden, R and Valentine, I (1984)
Learning to be a Capable Systems Agriculturalist
Programmed Learning & Educational Technology, 21, 4, 273–87.

The course described focuses not only on systems agriculturalists but also on those agriculturalists being autonomous learners and effective communicators, aimed at helping others and building up good interpersonal relationships. The course uses two learning strategies in two contexts. The contexts are staff initiative (gradually decreasing) and student initiative (gradually increasing); the latter involves the use of co-operative groups. The assessment is based around a student- and employer-initiated competency profile including peer and self-evaluation of learning.

Bejar, I I (1984)
Educational Diagnostic Assessment
Journal of Educational Measurement, 21, 2, 175–89.

The paper outlines the potential of microcomputers for enabling adaptive testing to improve the accuracy of self-referenced assessment. Two principal focuses of diagnostic assessment are noted: deficit measurement and error analysis. Deficit measurement focuses on areas where achievement is less than expected and has potential by using predictive strategies for present and future errors. Error analysis is seen as more clinical and less adapted to self-referencing. Error measurement is a problem for both styles of diagnostic assessment.

Boud, D (ed) (1981)
Developing Student Autonomy in Learning
London: Kogan Page.

Practising teachers working in higher education around the world describe their personal experiences of introducing alternatives to the traditional mode of teaching and course design. The issues of student, peer and teacher assessment are discussed. Case studies are given about the ways professional teachers have confronted the issues in areas such as independent study, self-directed learning and contract learning.

Boud, D and Lublin, J (1983)
Self Assessment in Professional Education
New South Wales, Australia: Tertiary Education Research Centre, University of New South Wales.

Outlines examples of self- and peer assessment and feedback in electrical engineering, law, architectural design and orthodontics. On the bases of the case studies and the attitudes of staff and students, the constraints and validity are considered. Suggestions are made for setting up such a procedure. There is an annotated bibliography of 126 items.

Buzan, T (1982)
Use Your Head
London: BBC Publications.

The book explains discoveries about the human brain and helps the reader to understand more clearly how his or her mind works. It includes tests and exercises to improve reading power, memory, studying effectively, solving problems more readily and ways of thinking. The well known mind maps (otherwise known as coral diagrams, patterned notes, etc) are a feature of the book.

European Community Action Programme: Transition of Young People from Education to Adult and Working Life (1984)
Education for Transition: The Curriculum Challenge
Brussels: Ifaplan.

The paper addresses five questions:

1. What competencies and knowledge will young people need?
2. How can they be motivated to attain them?
3. How can these competencies and this knowledge be learnt?
4. How do you start to make changes in these directions?
5. What are the other implications for financial and material

resources, staff development, and assessment and certification?

European Community Action Programme: Transition of Young People from Education to Adult and Working Life (1984)
New Developments in Assessment: Profiling (working document)
Brussels: Ifaplan.

The paper details two new developments in assessment and recording of assessment: student profiles, and personal records. The paper also discusses assessment and certification.

Gibbs, G (1981)
Teaching Students how to Learn: a Student Centred Approach
Milton Keynes: Open University Press.

The focus is on students learning from one another. By learning from peers with the same problems on the same course, the gap between them is less than that between most students and tutors. Examples are provided for carrying out the process, often using a snowballing approach.

Gibbs, G, Habeshaw, S and Habeshaw, T (1984)
53 Interesting Things To Do In Your Lectures
Bristol: Technical and Educational Services.

Describes a wide variety of techniques for use in lectures aimed at helping learners learn and become actively involved in their learning. In addition to techniques such as snowballing, the use of overhead projectors, handouts and tests are discussed.

Hand, J D (1984)
Student Development: The Next Logical Focus.
In Bass, R K and Dills, C R (eds) *Instructional Development: The State of the Art II*
Dubuque, Iowa: Kendall/Hunt.

A short paper outlining a theoretical basis for student development using learner's self-questioning focused around the learner's methods of learning and his or her life goals. The focus is towards life-oriented research and data gathering aimed at self-education. Examples are given for two universities in the USA.

Honey, P and Mumford, A (1982)
The Manual of Learning Styles
Maidenhead: Peter Honey.

A manual aimed particularly at managers, but of interest to all learners. The authors suggest four learning styles: activists, reflectors, theorists and pragmatists. The characteristics of all are

163

elaborated and a questionnaire is provided to enable a learner to classify his or her own style. The manual aims to enable learners to develop as all-rounders.

Huczynski, A (1983)
Encyclopaedia of Management Development Methods
Aldershot: Gower.

The title is indicative of a specific audience; however, it is likely that all educators and trainers will find much of relevance in this book. Some 300 methods of providing learning/teaching situations are outlined, generally with references to sources of more detailed information. In addition, a framework is provided to help teachers choose and analyse methods.

Jaques, D (1984)
Learning in Groups
London: Croom Helm.

The book addresses the questions: How can tutors in post-secondary education improve their skills in leading group discussions? How can the tutor play a less dominant role? How can students be encouraged to treat seminars as co-operative ventures? Theory and practice are linked by case studies including alternatives to the traditional tutorial and seminar.

Kitt, J (1984)
Schools of the Air and AUSSAT: Issues in Planning
Programmed Learning & Educational Technology, 21, 4, 318–23.

The paper outlines feasibility studies for upgrading current Schools of the Air facilities compared with enhanced facilities. The latter could incorporate satellite communications allowing a more interactive approach. The paper goes on to describe a particular strategy in one Australian state and how the pilot project is envisaged using ten families linked by satellite.

Knowles, M S (1973)
Self Directed Learning: A Guide for Teachers and Learners
New York: Associated Press.

Designed primarily for adult learners, the book provides a useful resource for all learners and their teachers who wish to place greater emphasis on learning being directed by the learner. The book provides many helpful hints, ideas and checklists to facilitate a change in emphasis from teaching to learning.

Merrill, M D (1984)
What is Learner Control?
In Bass, R K and Dills, C R (eds) *Instructional Development: The State of the Art II*
Dubuque, Iowa: Kendall/Hunt.

Many examples of learning assume that all students should receive identical instruction. This idea is either untenable or unsupported. The paper addresses the idea of enabling the students to decide on the various mediational tracks and which they will use. Several aspects of student-controlled instruction and display selection are received, and a model for display processing is developed.

Rogers, C R (1983)
Freedom to Learn for the 80's
Columbus: Charles E Merrill Publishing Company.

The book derives from an earlier book *Freedom to Learn*. The goals are to provide a climate of trust in the learning environment. Decision making is seen as participating and enabling students to build their confidence and self-esteem and to develop into lifelong learners. The teacher is seen as a facilitator. The book is aimed at fully functioning people, whether teachers or learners.

Rowntree, D (1977)
Assessing Students: How Shall We Know Them?
London: Harper and Row.

A comprehensive and original analysis of the reasons for, methods and effects of assessing learners. Rowntree is constructively critical of much current assessment used in education and suggests that the purposes be re-examined with greater focus on learning.

Rudduck, J (1978)
Learning Through Small Group Discussion
Guildford: SRHE.

The book is divided into seven chapters. Each chapter is written in two parts: the issues and the evidence. The book covers the range from students' roles and training students in small-group work to the leaders' roles; also included are monitoring small-group work and leaderless groups. The book covers a range of aspects from basic practical matters to more philosophical and psychological issues.

Appendix: Audioconferencing

What is audioconferencing?

Audioconferencing is simply meeting by telephone. Three or more people using their desk or home telephones are linked together by a bridge so that they can speak to each other. An ordinary telephone can be replaced by a loudspeaking telephone unit which plugs into the standard telephone jack socket and enables a group of people to participate from one site. The general term for the use of the telephone system in this way is 'teleconferencing' which includes audioconferencing.

Though the UK has come very recently to audioconferencing, particularly in education and training, other parts of the world, especially the USA and Australia, have made extensive use of audioconferencing media. The University of Wisconsin Extension has 35,000 students enrolled for courses which are delivered and tutored by audioconferencing. These include courses for beekeepers and pigeon breeders where the participants gather in a rural school house or in someone's parlour. In Alaska more than 3000 conferences a year are arranged by the Learn Alaska Network which reaches rural and island communities including Eskimo groups.

Problems of distance may not seem too serious in the UK, but even an urban journey to an evening class can be tortuous for anyone without a car. There is a growing use of audioconferencing for teaching and training. A Council for Educational Technology (CET) project in Ely used audioconferencing to link rural primary schools to share specialist teaching. A similar project linked sixth forms in North Wales to a local college to support small sociology groups which could not easily have functioned without this support. The potential for distance learning is enormous: the Open University has used the telephone for tutorials in Scotland with marked success. One participant who walks to a telephone box in all weathers to meet her fellow students on the air called this her 'course lifeline'!

Who can use audioconferencing?

There are a wide range of uses for audioconferencing including:

1. Courses held at more than one centre.
2. Distance learning at home or in groups.
3. Students on industrial placement. Students on placement can lose touch with their college and particularly with their fellow students. For example, advanced catering students in Brussels, Paris and Geneva have been put in touch with each other and with their tutor in the UK.
4. Expert inputs to courses. A group using a loudspeaking telephone can be addressed by an expert from anywhere in the world.
5. Conferences, meetings, etc. Audioconferencing can be used to improve the effectiveness of meetings. A half-hour session to agree an agenda or to discuss matters arising from a previous meeting facilitates business. Committee meetings can be held by telephone but they require particular care in preparation of papers and demand sensitive and positive chairing. Participants may welcome this discipline in that a one-hour meeting takes one hour — necessary decisions are made then, and there is no tendency to make the meeting last until the tea and biscuits arrive!
6. 'Phone-ins'. For example, experts on small businesses have been linked from their homes to a phone-in. A regular phone-in is available to students on an Open Tech electronics course. Though the students ring in with a specific query, feedback confirms that mutual support from other students is motivating for a student working alone from a package.

It is the interactive feature of audioconferencing that has most to offer to education and training. Rather than lecture by telephone, material (for example notes, guides, taped lectures, videotapes or computer software) can be sent by post and then queried, discussed and evaluated live.

The bandwidth of most normal telephone lines only permits either voice or data transmission at one time. More elaborate conferencing using television cameras to transmit live colour pictures normally uses special land links and satellites. There are some compromises in use or being explored at the present time. Black and white pictures can be transmitted over a single telephone line by a slow build-up technique known as slow scan or freeze-frame. The University of Essex is experimenting with a

167

simplified cartoon-style image which can be transmitted live. Links between a number of computer-controlled visual display units (eg, Excom 100) allow speech and data/pictorial information transfer using two telephone lines.

Bibliography

Abu-Sayf, F K (1979)
The Scoring of Multiple Choice Tests: A Closer Look
Educational Technology, 19, 6, 5–15.

Acres, D (1984)
Exams Without Anxiety: A Study Guide for Students, Parents and Other Helpers
Stoke on Trent: Deanhouse.

Anderson, S B and Ball, S (1978)
The Profession and Practice of Program Evaluation
San Francisco: Jossey Bass.

Arlin, M (1984)
Time, Equality and Mastery Learning
Review of Educational Research, 54, 1, 65–86.

Bannister, D and Fransella, F (1971)
Inquiring Man
Middlesex: Penguin Books.

Barnes, D (1976)
From Communication To Curriculum
London: Penguin Books.

Beard, R and Hartley, J (1984)
Teaching and Learning in Higher Education
London: Harper and Row.

Beck, J and Cox, C (eds) (1980)
Advances in Management Education
Chichester: Wiley.

Belbin, R N (1981)
Management Teams: Why They Succeed or Fail
London: Heinemann.

Biggs, J B and Collis, K F (1982)
Evaluating the Quality of Learning
New York: Academic Press.

Biggs, S (1980)
The Me I See: Acting, Participating, Observing and Viewing and
their Implications for Videofeedback
Human Relations, 33, 8, 575–88.

Black, H (1962)
They Shall Not Pass
New York: William Morrow.

Bloomfield, B A, Dobby, J L and Kendall, L (1979)
Ability and Examinations at 16 +
London: Macmillan.

Boydell, T and Pedler, M (1981)
Management Self Development: Concepts and Practices
Aldershot: Gower.

Brewer, I M (1979)
Group Teaching Strategies for Promoting Individual Skills in
Problem-Solving
Programmed Learning & Educational Technology, 16, 2, 111–28.

Bryce, J, Esdaile, S and Horan, M (1983)
A Criterion-Referenced Multiple-Choice Test Using Slides as
Cues
Programmed Learning & Educational Technology, 20, 4, 263–8.

Burstall, C and Kay, B (1978)
Assessment: The American Experience
London: HMSO.

Case, R and Bereiter, C (1984)
From Behaviourism to Cognitive Behaviourism to Cognitive
Development: Steps in the Evolution of Instructional Design
Instructional Science, 13, 141–58.

Chausarkar, B A (1983)
On Attitudes to a Method of Assessment
Learning Systems Bulletin, 7, 1, 19–23.

Chausarkar, B A and Rautroy, U (1981)
How Relevant is Continuous Assessment?: a Business Studies
Experience
Assessment in Higher Education, 1, 6, 49–56.

Choppin, B H and McArthur, D L (1984)
Computerised Diagnostic Testing
Journal of Educational Measurement, 21, 4, 391–7.

Clements, R (1980)
A Guide to Transactional Analysis: A Handbook For Managers and Trainers
London: Insight Training.

Clift, P, Macintosh, H and Nuttall, D (1981)
Measuring Learning Outcomes
Milton Keynes: Open University Press.

Cohen, L and Manion, L (1985)
Research Methods in Education
London: Croom Helm.

Davies, E R (1976)
The Role of Self-Paced Study in Undergraduate Science Teaching
British Journal of Educational Technology, 7, 3, 23–40.

Davies, W J K (1980)
Alternatives to Class Teaching in Schools and Colleges
London: Council for Educational Technology.

Denham, C H (1975)
Criterion Referenced, Domain Referenced and Norm-referenced Measurement: a Parallax View
Educational Technology, 42, 9–13.

Depres, D (1980)
A Study Assignment Approach to Training
Journal of European Industrial Training, 4, 3, 14–16.

Dundas-Grant, V (1975)
Attainment at 16 + : The French Perspective
Comparative Education, 1, 13–22.

Evans, C (1980)
The Use of Student Led Groups or Syndicates in French Literature Classes
British Journal of Educational Technology, 11, 3, 185–200.

Feletti, G I (1984)
Assessment for Capability
Programmed Learning & Educational Technology, 21, 4, 294–300.

171

FEU (1982)
Profiles: a Review of Issues and Practice in the Use and Development of Student Profiles
London: Further Education Unit.

FEU (1984)
Profiles in Action
London: Further Education Unit.

Forsyth, J P and Dockerell, W B (1979)
Curriculum and Assessment for 14 to 16 Year Olds in Scottish Secondary Schools
Edinburgh: SCRE.

Fox, D (1983)
Personal Theories of Teaching
Studies in Higher Education, 8, 2, 151–63.

Fox, R, Luszki, M B and Schmuck, R (1966)
Diagnosing Classroom Learning Environments
Chicago: Science Research Associates.

Francis, J (1982)
A Case For Open Book Examinations
Educational Review, 34, 1, 13–26.

Glaser, B and Strauss, A (1970)
Discovery of Grounded Theory
Chicago: Markham.

Goacher, B (1983)
Recording Achievement at 16 +
London: Longman, Schools Council.

Harlen, W, Darwin, A and Murphy, M (1977)
Match and Mismatch: Raising Questions
Edinburgh: Oliver & Boyd.

Heron, J (1977)
Dimensions of Facilitator Style
Guildford: University of Surrey.

Heron, J (1981)
Self and Peer Assessment.
In Boydell, T and Pedler, M (eds) *Management Self Development: Concepts and Practices*
Aldershot: Gower.

Holmberg, B (1981)
Status and Trends of Distance Education
London: Kogan Page.

Holt, M (1981)
Evaluating the Evaluators
Sevenoaks: Hodder and Stoughton.

Hudson, B (1973)
Assessment Techniques: An Introduction
London: Methuen.

Jonassen, D H (1984)
Developing a Learning Strategy Using Pattern Notes: a New
Technology
Programmed Learning & Educational Technology, 21, 3, 163–75.

Kandaswamy, S (1980)
Evaluation of Instructional Materials: A Synthesis of Models and
Methods
Educational Technology, 20, 6, 19–26.

Kellington, S H and Mitchel, A C (1980)
Designing an Assessment System on the Principles of Criterion
Referenced Measurement
School Science Review, 61, 217, 765–70.

Kemmis, S (1978)
Nomothetic and Ideographic Approaches to the Evaluation of
Learning
Journal of Curriculum Studies, 10, 1, 45–59.

Lacey, C and Lawton D (eds) (1981)
Issues in Evaluation and Accountability
London: Methuen.

Lewis, R (1984)
*How To Help Learners Assess Their Progress: Writing Objectives, Self
Assessment Questions and Activities*
London: Council for Educational Technology.

Lyman, H B (1978)
Test Scores and What They Mean
Englewood Cliffs, New Jersey: Prentice Hall.

McCormic, R (1981)
Analysing Curriculum Materials
Milton Keynes: Open University Press.

McCormic, R (1982)
Approaches to Evaluation: Audited Self-Evaluation
Milton Keynes: Open University Press.

Macintosh, H G (ed) (1974)
Techniques and Problems of Assessment
London: Edward Arnold.

Main, A (1980)
Encouraging Effective Learning
Edinburgh: Scottish Academic Press.

Marland, M (1981)
Information Skills in the Secondary Curriculum
London: Methuen Educational.

Mathias, H and Rutherford, D (1982)
Lecturers as Evaluators: the Birmingham Experience
Studies in Higher Education, 7, 1, 47–56.

Ments, M van (1983)
The Effective Use of Role-Play: A Handbook for Teachers and Trainers
London: Kogan Page.

Mevarech, Z R and Shulamit, W (1985)
Are Mastery Learning Strategies Beneficial for Developing
Problem Solving Skills?
Higher Education, 14, 4, 425–32.

Miller, A H (1978)
Analysing Teaching in Student Centred Classrooms
British Journal of Teacher Education, 4, 1, 37–45.

Mitroff, I and Kilmann, R H (1978)
Methodological Approaches to Social Science
San Francisco: Jossey Bass.

Morris, J (1971)
Management Development and Developmental Management
Personnel Review, 1, 1, 30–43.

Mumford, A (1980)
Making Experience Pay
London: McGraw Hill.

NFER (1976)
*Criterion Referenced Measurement and Criterion Referenced Tests: Review
of Published Work 1960–1975*
Slough: NFER.

Pedler, M (1974)
Learning in Management Education
Journal of European Training, 3, 3, 182–94.

Pine, G J and Boy, A V (1977)
Learner-Centred Teaching: A Humanistic View
Colorado: Love Publishing.

Postman, N and Weingartner, C (1971)
Teaching as a Subversive Activity
London: Penguin Books.

Romiszowski, A J (1984)
Producing Instructional Systems: Lesson Planning for Individualized and Group Learning Activities
London: Kogan Page.

Shayer, M and Adey, P (1981)
Towards a Science of Science Teaching
London: Heinemann.

Smith, N L (1981)
Evaluating Evaluation Methods
Studies in Educational Evaluation, 7, 2, 173–81.

Smith, P B (1980)
Group Processes and Personal Change
London: Harper and Row.

Suessmuth, P (1978)
Ideas for Training Managers and Supervisors
Mansfield: University Associates of Europe.

Tait, K and Hughes, I E (1984)
Some Experiences in Using a Computer Based Learning System as an Aid to Self Teaching and Self Assessment.
Computers and Education, 8, 3, 271–8.

Tenbrink, T (1974)
Evaluation: A Practical Guide for Teachers
New York: McGraw Hill.

Thomas, L F and Harri-Augstein, S (1985)
Self Organised Learning: Foundations of a Conversational Science for Psychology
London: Routledge and Kegan Paul.

Tough, A (1979)
The Adult's Learning Projects
Toronto: Ontario Institute for Studies in Education.

Walstad, W B (1984)
Analysing Minimal Competency Test Performance
Journal of Educational Research, 77, 5, 261–6.

Warren, J R (1971)
College Grading Practices: An Overview
Washington: ERIC Clearinghouse.

Webb, G (1981)
An Evaluation of Techniques for Analysing Small Group Work
Programmed Learning & Educational Technology, 18, 2, 64–6.

Wessells, M G (1982)
Cognitive Psychology
New York: Harper and Row.

Winter-Hebron, C (1983)
Performance Evaluation of Teaching: a Diagnostic Approach
Higher Education in Europe, 8, 2, 5–17.

Wood, R and Napthali, W A (1975)
Assessment in the Classroom: What do Teachers Look For?
Educational Studies, 1, 151–61.

Zeitlin, N and Goldberg, A C (1970)
Structural Communications: Interactive System for Teaching Understanding
Training Technology, 10, 6, 51–9.

Index

KING ALFRED'S COLLEGE
LIBRARY

179